MASTER YOUR TIME

A PRACTICAL GUIDE TO INCREASE YOUR
PRODUCTIVITY AND USE YOUR TIME
MEANINGFULLY

THIBAUT MEURISSE

Edited by
KERRY J DONOVAN

CONTENTS

How many of your goals and dreams have you postponed due to a perceived lack of time?

Nowadays, everybody is busy. We never seem to find enough time to focus on the things that really matter to us. We tell ourselves our dreams are not important. We postpone our vision, using the same excuse over and over, "I can always do it tomorrow." But tomorrow never arrives. And as the years pass, our dreams slowly fade until they are completely forgotten.

We neglect our friends and family and take our relationships for granted. We can always spend time with them later. We can show them our appreciation later. We can catch up later, right?

But time is ruthless.

Each second only comes once. We can never go back in time and reclaim the thousands of hours we wasted on meaningless activities. And we have no idea how much time we have left.

But time is also a blessing. It's a gift that comes to us second by second. And we always have the opportunity to use that gift in a meaningful way—in a way that reflects our deepest values and our greatest aspirations.

How can we ensure that we're using our time meaningfully and in a way that minimizes regrets and makes it worthwhile?

This is what we're going to explore throughout this book.

In *Master Your Time*, I'll invite you to reflect on the way you're spending your time. By doing so, you'll be able to use your time more meaningfully and more effectively.

More specifically, you'll learn:

- What productivity truly means and how it works,
- How procrastination works and how to overcome it,
- The one myth that prevents you from mastering your time,
- How to create a productivity system that works for *you* so that you can stick to it long-term,

- The seven criteria that will ensure you use your time meaningfully both at work and in your personal life,
- How to reclaim thousands of hours of your time and utilize them to achieve your goals and dreams, and more.

If any of the above points pique your interest, read on.

INTRODUCTION

We all have twenty-four hours in every day. Yet some people use their time to accomplish extraordinary things, while others accomplish very little with it. Why is that?

It's because most people fail to value their time. They tell themselves they can always do what they want tomorrow, acting as though time was an abundant commodity. In reality, time is one of the scarcest resources on earth. We can produce more of almost anything by adding more labor and/or capital, but we can never create more time.

Each second you spend on unproductive activities is forever lost. You can *never* reclaim those precious seconds. The simple truth is this:

Whenever you choose to dedicate time to one activity, you implicitly say no to everything else you could be doing at that time. Think of how many thousands of hours you may have spent watching TV, for example.

This time is gone forever.

You could have dedicated it to working toward meaningful goals and exciting dreams—but you didn't. And when you keep squandering your time in such a way, you will end up living a life that is not the one you really desire.

Most people fail to grasp the true value of time. If they did, they would spend their day very differently. Fortunately, we can all learn to value our time more highly. And as we do so, we will inevitably design a more meaningful life.

What about you? Are you treating time as your most valuable asset? Are you using it each day to move closer to your dreams? Or are you casual with time, behaving as though it is infinite?

Many people envy the investor, Warren Buffet, who is one of the richest men in the world. But I'd rather be me, four years ago when I was an unknown author, losing money with my business. Why? Because back then, I had an asset that Warren Buffet could never buy. I had something much scarcer than money.

I had time!

I had decades ahead of me (and still have—hopefully).

Now, think about this:

Would you rather be in the shoes of Warren Buffet or in your own shoes? Would you rather have time or money?

In truth, you're probably wealthier than Warren Buffet. While he is money rich, you are time rich. And if you use your time well, you will be able to achieve many of your goals in the coming years.

Do you realize now how valuable your time is?

I only started taking serious action toward my dreams when I learned how valuable my time truly was. From that point on, instead of wasting my time, I began to make every moment count. Armed with a simple pen and a sheet of paper, I sat down and wrote where I wanted to be in five years. Then, I set goals and took action every day to ensure I was making progress toward them.

Today, five years later, most of my goals have become reality. I'm now a full-time writer and have sold over two hundred thousand books worldwide. And I did it in a highly competitive market, in a foreign language (foreign to me).

Needless to say, I had to overcome my fair share of self-doubt in the process. However, I did understand that, even if I didn't take any action toward my goals, those five years would pass anyway. As such, I determined to make the most of the time, in the hopes of ending up where I wanted to be after the five years had passed.

You can do the same. You too can achieve wonderful goals.

But everything starts by truly valuing your time. If you can learn to value your time, you will be able to reach your dreams and live a meaningful life. By using your valuable time wisely, over the long term, you will achieve more than you can possibly imagine.

Throughout this book, we'll explore in depth how you can use your time more effectively, which will enable you to experience a deeper sense of fulfillment and achieve most of your goals. In truth, highly productive people are often no smarter than the majority, but they have discovered the true value of time. Seeing every single day as a new opportunity, these productive people make daily progress toward their goals.

Would you like to discover how to use your time well so that you can achieve almost anything you desire?

The choice is yours.

In this book, we'll cover the following topics.

In **Part I. Understanding Productivity**, we'll talk about productivity and what it really is. We'll see why most productivity systems fail and why you should probably stop reading so many books on productivity.

In **Part II. Changing Your Perception of Time**, we'll discuss how your current perception of time may lead you to make poor use of your time (and what you can do about it).

In **Part III. Making a Meaningful Use of Your Time,** we'll see what you can do to use your time wisely by introducing a simple framework that will help you identify what matters most to you.

In **Part IV. Making an Effective Use of Your Time,** we'll see how to enhance your productivity and ensure you use your time as effectively as possible.

In **Part V. Developing Extraordinary Focus**, we'll discuss how you can develop exceptional focus and boost your concentration dramatically. You'll learn why increasing your level of focus is key when it comes to expanding your productivity.

So, are you ready to become the master of your time?

If so, let's get started.

Your Free Step-By-Step Workbook

To help you master your time I've created a workbook as a companion guide to this book. I highly encourage you to download it at the following URL:

http://whatispersonaldevelopment.org/master-your-time

I'll also send you a free eBook. It will help you tremendously on your personal development journey.

If you have any difficulties downloading the workbook contact me at:

thibaut.meurisse@gmail.com and I will send it to you as soon as possible.

Alternatively, you can also use the workbook available at the end of this book.

Master Your Life With The Mastery Series

This book is the eighth book in the *Mastery Series*. You can check out the first book, *Master Your Emotions* at the URL below:

http://mybook.to/Master_Emotions

What readers say about *Master Your Emotions*:

"I am a psychologist and I love this book because of it's simplicity. It is so easy to read and understand. I will be referring many of my clients to download this book." -- Laura Beth Cooper, Ph.D., Psychologist

"Changed my life"

"This book kept me all the way to the end! I couldn't put it down and when I did I couldn't wait to pick it up again!"

"One of the best self help books I have ever read!"

"This will be one of my go to books, like How to Win Friends and Influence People, Start with Why, and a handful of others that I will continuously go back to."

PART I

UNDERSTANDING PRODUCTIVITY

1

THE IMPORTANCE OF MEANING

Becoming a master of y our time involves using your time more productively. But what does this mean? Unless we define exactly what is meant by "being more productive" we cannot advance our discussion. So, let's take a moment to discuss productivity. Here, I define productivity as:

Doing the things we enjoy or find meaningful, while being around people we care about.

You cannot be a master of your time if you spend the majority of your day doing things you find meaningless while, at the same time, wishing you could be somewhere else, with someone else, doing something else.

Sure, you can be the most productive employee in your company, but if you'd rather be anywhere else but in the office, are you truly productive on a personal level?

Now, in this case, finding "meaning" doesn't require you to find pleasure or enjoyment in every task or role. You can find meaning in challenging situations. For instance, a job might be difficult, but it can also allow you to provide for your family and offer a bright future to your children. It might be stressful, but it might also give you a sense of contribution. Or it might be boring but enable you to have positive social interactions with your colleagues or clients.

In short, being a master of your time doesn't necessarily mean having the freedom to do whatever you want, whenever you want, while avoiding any serious commitment. Such "freedom" can often be devoid of meaning. In fact, I believe that meaning comes precisely from having a sense of commitment toward someone and/or something.

Also, I'm not telling you to quit your job today. However, I do invite you to use the things you learn in this book to reflect on your life and on how you're currently spending your time. If your goal is to become more productive at work, that's fine. If you aspire to use your personal time more effectively, that's fine too. This book will help you either way.

The second element is having meaningful relationships. On their deathbed, nobody wishes they had watched more series on Netflix, spent more time scrolling their Facebook newsfeed, or posted more pictures of themselves on Instagram. Yet, most of us spend an incredible amount of time doing exactly that. Instead, we'll probably wish we had spent more time with our family and friends, right?

According to a nurse who recorded the most common regrets of her dying patients, one of their biggest misgivings was that they didn't stay in touch with their friends. Caught up in their busy lives, they failed to nurture relationships with people they cared about. What about you? If you were to die today, what relationships do you regret allowing to wither?

The point is, when you spend time with people you're close to while being fully *in the present*, you can say you're using your time effectively.

The third element is doing things you enjoy, whether it is at work or in your personal life. And I don't mean playing video games all day, eating junk food, or watching amusing videos on YouTube. What I'm talking about here is engaging in activities that nourish your soul. For some, it might be writing. For others, it might be dancing. Yet for others, it might be building something with their hands. When you engage in such activities, you often lose track of time. This is a sign that you are being productive in your own way.

To sum up, one of the keys to becoming the master of your time is to develop a deeper sense of *meaning* in your life. When you find meaning in your work, develop meaningful relationships and cultivate hobbies that make you feel alive, you'll be aware that you are using your time more effectively.

Think about it this way:

When you reach the end of your time on earth, you won't assess your life based on how much money you made or how big your house was. Instead, you'll assess your time on this earth based upon whether your life was meaningful and worth living.

Therefore, I encourage you to ponder the following question:

"What meaningful things do I need to work on today, this week, or this year to obtain the approval of my future self?"

Such a deep question should not be answered casually or once only. It should be considered carefully and reviewed on a regular basis.

So, what meaningful things do you need to start doing more of today?

Action step

Using your action guide, assess how meaningfully you're using your time right now, both at work and in your personal life.

2

PRODUCTIVITY ISN'T ONLY ABOUT TIME MANAGEMENT

While this book is entitled, *Master Your Time*, the truth is that being productive isn't purely about managing your time effectively. It's actually about managing your activities, and the level of intensity you approach them with, more productively.

Let me explain.

First, the value of an hour of your time fluctuates. For instance, you might have more energy in the morning than you do in the evening, after work. As a result, one "morning hour" might be much more valuable than one "evening hour". In fact, it may be two, or even three times more valuable! Consequently, by not using this hour effectively, you're significantly hindering your levels of productivity. In short, productivity is not only about time, but also about the level of energy you have available *during* that time.

Second, an hour of your time will be worth more if you put more intensity into what you do during that hour. For instance, imagine that I decide to spend one hour working on this book in the morning but, every five minutes, I check my phone or my inbox. Under these conditions, how much is that hour of my time truly worth? Thirty minutes? Fifteen minutes? Five minutes? It's hard to say, but it's definitely not the full sixty minutes. Put another way, to be fully productive you must put your *undivided focus* on the task at hand.

Third, the value of an hour of your time is heavily dependent on the tasks you perform during that time. The more these tasks fit into the big picture—i.e., the goals you're trying to accomplish—the more productive you'll become. And the clearer your vision or strategy is, the better you'll be able to identify the key tasks you must work on.

Fourth, the value of an hour of your time depends upon your level of excitement. If you enjoy doing something, you'll have more energy and, as a result, you will be more productive. You'll have no problem motivating yourself and will be less likely to become distracted. This is why people who are passionate about what they do, can persevere for years and may appear to have far more energy than other people. The more passionate and excited you are about what you do, the better.

As you can see, productivity is more about making sure you're working on the right task with the right level of energy and focus than it is about completing an extended to-do list.

What about you? How well are you using the energy you have during the day?

The energy cycle described in the next section will help you understand how energy works and how you can use it to enhance your productivity.

Action step

Using your action guide, write down how well you're using your time. Answer the following statements using a scale from 1 to 10 (one being false, ten being true):

1. I make the most of my peak hours each day.
2. I work on each task with focus while eliminated distractions.
3. The tasks I work on usually move me closer to my long-term goals.
4. I'm excited about most of the tasks I'm working on.

The energy cycle and its six phases

Your productivity level depends on your energy level and how effectively you can channel your energy toward activities that matter. Below are the different phases of the energy cycle:

1. Protect energy. Your energy is limited, and the best way to protect it is to increase the quality of your sleep, eat more healthily and exercise more regularly. When you fail to do so, your available energy decreases.

2. Channel energy. Energy that is not directed toward a specific purpose will dissipate and be of little value. Once that energy dissipates, you'll *never* be able to get it back. Therefore, make sure the way you use your energy today helps you move closer to your ideal future life. To do so, you need a clear vision and a sound strategy.

3. Allocate energy. You don't have enough energy to do everything at once. According to the 80/20 Principle, twenty percent of your activities will generate eighty percent of your results. Using this principle, make sure you focus on the tasks that absolutely matter.

4. Invest energy. Your energy must be invested otherwise it will be lost. Once you've identified your key tasks, put all your energy into them while eliminating any distractions.

5. Refill energy. Take breaks regularly so as to maintain good energy levels.

6. Restart the cycle. You can then restart the cycle all over again the following day.

The point is, the more you can preserve energy and channel it toward the achievement of your most important goals, the more productive you'll become.

Now, let's go over the five levels of productivity to give you a better idea of how productivity works.

3

THE FIVE LEVELS OF PRODUCTIVITY

I have defined five levels that capture the most important components of productivity. Understanding each of these levels will help you use your time more effectively. Think of them as the building blocks you can use to construct an effective system. Level one is the most fundamental level. As such, this is the one we'll focus upon almost exclusively in this book.

Below is a quick overview of each level.

Level 1—destroying distractions and improving your focus

Level one is about eliminating distractions and putting your undivided attention into your major task. Of course, how much uninterrupted focus you can generate during your day will vary greatly based on your job and your family situation. You might struggle to free just forty-five minutes, or you might be able to spend most of your day free of distractions. Any amount of time you manage to free up will be beneficial and is worth striving for.

Level 2—increasing your level of energy

Level two is about increasing your energy. To boost your productivity further, you must channel all your energy into the completion of your key task(s). This will enable you to inject more intensity into your time and to accomplish more as a result. With more energy, you'll also be able to focus for longer. Finally, having more energy will make any activity you engage in more enjoyable, whether you are spending quality time with your family, indulging in your hobbies or working on your side hustle. To increase your overall energy levels, you must focus on the fundamentals. These fundamentals are: eating well, sleeping well and exercising regularly.

Level 3—clarifying your long-term vision

This level is about focusing on the correct things. You can complete as many tasks as you like, but if they don't move you closer to your goals, what's the point? This is why you must clarify your vision to ensure that what you do today is aligned with where you want to be tomorrow.

Bear in mind that, while I put it as level three, in truth, this is fundamental to your long-term productivity. However, I propose that, in the short term, you're better off cultivating your ability to focus.

As a bare minimum, make sure you answer the fifteen questions introduced in **Part III. Making a Meaningful Use of Your Time** — *4. Being productive the right way*. This will help you gain clarity. Alternatively, you can also read book three in this series, *Master Your Focus*, which addresses this topic in greater depth.

Level 4—planning your day effectively

This level is about optimizing your system and becoming a more effective planner. Through effective planning you can reduce distractions and increase the amount of focus you have available throughout the day.

In **Part V. Developing an Extraordinary Focus**, we'll discuss how to work effectively using the CEO/COO/employee framework.

Level 5—having an active social life and building meaningful relationships

The fifth level is about building meaningful relationships. How often and how well we interact with others has a big impact on our levels of productivity.

I learned about this first-hand when I quit my job in Japan and moved back in with my parents while I was building my business. During that time, my productivity wasn't optimal. I was taking long breakfasts, lunches and dinners with my parents when I could have been working. I imagined how much more I could do if I lived by myself (I was in a period of transition looking for places from which I could operate my business). Despite this, during the year I stayed with my parents I wrote seven books, which is no mean feat.

Then, in early 2019, I moved to Estonia and expected to have much more time to work and write many more books.

Well, that's not at all what happened.

That year, I ended up writing only three books. Of course, many factors could explain why my productivity dropped. But I believe one key element was that I was living alone and didn't have much of a social life.

Studies have shown that social interactions have a direct impact on productivity. This is because humans aren't machines. We can't just work and neglect everything else (hobbies, sleep, diet, social life, et cetera). We need balance in our lives if we are to maintain optimal productivity.

My point is, don't neglect your social life. By meeting new people, or keeping in touch with friends and family, you're not *spending* your time, you're *investing* it, both by developing meaningful interactions and by increasing your overall productivity.

I put socializing as level five, assuming you already have some kind of social life. However, if you don't, consider making it a higher priority. It could significantly boost your productivity.

So, what level do you relate to the most?

Most people are at level one. That is, they're constantly distracted whether internally (by their thoughts), or externally (by their phone, social media, emails, et cetera). As a result, they struggle to focus hard enough and for long enough to complete their most important tasks. Since you're reading this book, you're probably in a similar situation.

This is why we'll focus on getting level one right throughout this book.

On a side note, focusing on level one doesn't mean you should ignore level two and fail to exercise, eat loads of junk food and neglect your sleep. Nor does it suggest you should spend no time thinking of your vision (level three), planning your day (level four), or socializing (level five). It simply means that you should direct most of your energy toward enhancing your focus, while keeping other levels as they are —for now.

4

PRODUCTIVITY DOESN'T REQUIRE COMPLEX SYSTEMS

The only productivity system that will work for you is the one you can maintain over the long term. If your system isn't sustainable, it won't be successful.

Below are a couple of tips to help you build an effective system.

A. Forget about productivity tools

I don't really believe in productivity tools. If anything, they are yet another distraction that prevents you from doing the real work. Sure, some productivity tools can be useful, but unless you're already extremely productive, they won't do much for you. In most cases, planning and strategizing using pen and paper is more than enough.

B. Think in terms of productivity levels, not systems

A more effective way to think of productivity is as a ladder you learn to climb over time. Some productivity systems are more complex than others. While they may work for people who are already highly productive, they probably don't work for most people. Thus, if such systems failed to work for you in the past, don't feel guilty. Just start with a simpler one. You can implement more advanced systems later if you need to.

In this book, I will share a few specific things you can do to turbocharge your productivity. For instance, one of them is to develop a consistent habit of focusing single-mindedly on one task for a long period while eliminating any distraction. This is the first block upon which you can build a more advanced productivity system later on.

Next, we'll talk about procrastination and see how you can overcome your tendency to avoid work.

* * *

Action step

Using your action guide, write down what your current productivity system is (if you have one). Is it working for you? If not, how can you make it simpler and more effective?

WHAT IS PROCRASTINATION AND HOW TO OVERCOME IT

Let's face it. We all procrastinate from time to time. But, if you're a chronic procrastinator, this section will be essential to your development.

To overcome procrastination, you must first understand how motivation actually works and exactly why you procrastinate. Once you do so, it will become easier for you to let go of this disempowering habit.

I believe we procrastinate for the following reasons:

1. A lack of clarity
2. Insufficient awareness
3. Poor focus
4. Fear
5. Lack of urgency
6. Lack of effective routines
7. Unnecessary friction
8. Mental overload

Let's have a look at each of these elements in greater depth. As we go through the list, try to identify the main reason(s) you may be procrastinating in your life.

A. A lack of clarity

Lacking clarity means that you're unsure about:

- Why the task matters,
- Precisely what you need to do, and/or
- Exactly how you should approach the task.

a) You're unsure about why the task matters.

If you're given a task and can't see how it fits into the bigger picture or why it matters, you'll find it hard to develop the motivation required to work on it. This is why you must identify the specific reason(s) you're working on it. If you keep procrastinating, ask yourself whether you believe the task is truly important. If you can't find a convincing answer:

- Develop specific reasons to do it (strengthen your why). You can write down your answers to help you do this.
- Think of what will happen long term if you don't complete the task. What are the negative consequences?
- Visualize how good you'll feel about yourself once you've completed the task.
- Just get started while reminding yourself that the task is probably easier than you think.

b) You're not sure about what you need to do.

Another reason you may procrastinate is that you lack clarity regarding what needs to be done. Unable to picture the end result, you experience inner resistance, and this, in turn, prevents you from starting.

Ask yourself:

- Do I know exactly what I'm trying to accomplish?
- Can I picture the end results?

If not, try the following:

- Take a piece of paper and write down exactly what you're trying to do, and/or
- Ask your supervisors to give you more detail and clarify what they expects from you.

The more clarity you have regarding what needs to be done, the easier it will be to start working.

c) You're unsure exactly how you should approach the task.

Perhaps you know what the end result looks like but have no idea how to get there. Not knowing how to approach the task will also create inner resistance and lead to procrastination. When you're in this situation, try the following:

- Write down a specific plan to achieve the task.
- Ask someone who has already accomplished a similar task to help you define the best approach.
- Search online for hints on how to approach the task as effectively as possible.

As you can see, often you don't procrastinate because you're lazy, but because you lack clarity. To sum up, whenever you find yourself procrastinating over a specific task make sure you know:

- Why you must complete it,
- Exactly what the end product should look like, and
- How to approach the task effectively.

B. Insufficient awareness

The act of procrastination indicates that you have mental roadblocks and an inner resistance stopping you from doing your work. But it also means you may not fully understand how procrastination works.

Lacking awareness means that:

- You fail to understand how motivation works,
- You're unaware of the mental roadblocks that lead you to procrastinate, and/or
- You're holding onto erroneous mental models.

a) You fail to understand how motivation works.

Motivation isn't some magical tool you must possess before you can solve all your productivity issues.

In truth, action usually *creates* motivation. This means you don't necessarily need to feel motivated in order to do anything. This is what we call the motivation myth. If you buy into this myth, you'll end up procrastinating more and more often. You'll keep telling yourself that you will take action when you have more motivation.

However, this type of reasoning is flawed. It is called "emotional reasoning". Emotional reasoning is when you assume you must feel a certain way before you can do anything. If this were true, we would all be in big trouble. No, you don't need to feel like doing something to actually do it. For example:

- You don't need to feel confident enough to ask for a promotion,
- You don't need to be confident in your writing in order to publish a book, and
- You don't need to feel like studying in order to study.

Often, we refer to the action of doing something when not feeling as though you want to as "being disciplined". However, perhaps another way to frame it would be as "acting in alignment with reality"—the reality that an extraordinary amount of motivation isn't required before we can act.

The point is, you don't need to feel like it to do something. Instead, you need to act, and as you do so, you'll feel more and more motivated as you continue.

b) You're unaware of the mental roadblocks that lead you to procrastinate

If you're procrastinating right now it means that there are mental obstacles standing in your way. Consequently, rather than trying harder or beating yourself up, why not identify what these obstacles are?

Some examples of common obstacles are:

- Making your tasks far bigger in your mind than they actually are.
- Not being fully convinced you should be working on the task. Perhaps it goes against your values. Perhaps there is something else you want to do instead. Or perhaps you think the timing isn't right.

To help you overcome your roadblocks, try the following actions:

- Chunk down your task until it's so small that you can start working on it without resistance.
- Using a pen and paper, answer the following questions:

1. "What exactly prevents me from working on this task?", and
2. "What would it require for me to be sold on this task?"

c) You have erroneous mental models

Our brain is mostly designed to ensure our survival so that we can reproduce and pass on our genes. As such, it is reluctant to spend energy unless it perceives a life-threatening situation. When it recognizes we're safe, it will try to maintain the status quo rather than seeking discomfort or uncertainty.

When our ancestors had to protect themselves against the cold, they didn't procrastinate on making clothes to keep them warm. However, today, we can usually put off our tasks for ages before anything threatening happens. And, in most cases, nothing of the sort ever will. We'll just feel bad, knowing we're letting ourselves down. But we will survive.

The bottom line is that people who let their "old" brain dictate their actions are merely surviving. To stop procrastinating, you must decide, not just to survive, but to thrive. Thriving involves moving beyond your comfort zone and doing what needs to be done whether you feel like it or not (i.e., aligning yourself with reality rather than being a slave of your feelings).

Yet another reason you put things off is that you hold onto a disempowering perception of procrastination. When you procrastinate, you ignore the present moment—the only thing real—and ask an imagined self to deal with future tasks. By doing so, you're effectively unloading your burden onto a future self who doesn't exist. There are a couple of major problems with this approach:

1. **You can only act in the present.** When you refuse to act now and transfer your responsibility to a future self instead, you give up on a precious opportunity to accomplish your duty in the only moment that is real—the present moment. The time you fail to use effectively is lost forever.
2. **Your future self is the result of your current self, who is acting in the present.** When you postpone a task to a later date, you effectively buy into the myth that your future self will be wiser, stronger, smarter or more motivated than your present self. However, this is illogical. Your future self will only be wiser, stronger, smarter or more motivated if you *actively* work on becoming those things in the present.

The bottom line is this. When you procrastinate, you disrespect the present moment and believe that, in an illusory future, you will be more disciplined. Life simply doesn't work that way.

Instead, learn to act now so that your future self *does* become smarter, better, stronger and wiser. This is the key to achieving everything you desire.

C. Poor focus

These days, focus has become an increasingly rare commodity. Most people can't work for more than a few minutes before being interrupted or distracting themselves. Dozens of times during the day, people check their phones, go on social media or read news updates. While this is a major problem, it's by no means the biggest one.

The major issue is that, these days, we tend to be overstimulated. By constantly checking our phones, reading our emails or scrolling through our social media newsfeeds, we put ourselves in a state of overstimulation. Such a state makes it difficult to work on unappealing or challenging tasks. We may genuinely *want* to work on these tasks, but for some reason, we can't.

Later in this book, we'll discover what you can do to eliminate distractions and lower your level of stimulation.

D. Fear

The biggest thing holding you back might be the fear of not doing a good enough job. If so, the first step forward is to acknowledge your fear.

Remember, being afraid of doing something doesn't mean you shouldn't or can't do it. This is flawed thinking. In truth, many of the most talented people on this planet, feel like failures. Read the two quotes below to get an idea of what I mean.

 When I won the Oscar, I thought it was a fluke. I thought everybody would find out, and they'd take it back. They'd come to my house, knocking on the door, 'Excuse me, we meant to give that to someone else. That was going to Meryl Streep.'

— JODIE FOSTER, ACTOR.

You think, 'Why would anyone want to see me again in a movie? And I don't know how to act anyway, so why am I doing this?'

— MERYL STREEP, ACTOR.

So, what should you do?

While there are many things you can do to deal with feelings of inadequacy better, the first step is simply to think along these lines:

"I might feel as though I'm inadequate for the rest of my life, but so what? I'm going to see any meaningful projects through to the end anyway."

The way I see it, you have two choices:

1. Experience feelings of inadequacy and let them stop you from completing your tasks, or

2. Experience feelings of inadequacy but strive to accomplish everything you set your mind to the best you can anyway.

Whichever choice you make, your future will unfold in a completely different way.

Your feelings of inadequacy may or may not diminish. Even if they don't, so what?

Below are some things you can do to alleviate your feelings of inadequacy:

- **Realize you're exactly where you supposed to be *right now*.** You're always doing the best you can with what you have (as is any other human being). Therefore, give yourself credit for it.
- **Understand you can always improve.** Think of your life as a journey, not a destination. Then, do the task in front of you to the best of your ability, knowing you will inevitably get better with practice.
- **Adopt the identity of a learner.** Stop tell yourself you'll

finally be good enough once you achieve X, Y or Z—which is a complete fantasy—and enjoy every tiny bit of progress you make along the way. Take pride in being a learner. Enjoy making progress and learning new things just for the sake of it. You'll only ever know an infinitesimal fraction of everything there is to know, anyway.

- **Realize you can never be "good enough".** Shift the paradigm. Let go of the idea that you *can* or *should* be good enough. You cannot win that game. At what point exactly can you say you're good enough? How will you measure your level of "good-enoughness"? And for how long will it last? This paradigm doesn't work and will create a great deal of suffering.

To conclude, do what you have to do, whether you feel good enough or not. You might not be as good as you want to be (yet) in some areas of your life. However, you'll inevitably improve with practice over time. And that's where the fun is. So, learn to enjoy the journey. Rejoice in learning new things about yourself or about the world, and complete the task in front of you the best way you can.

E. No feeling of urgency

What will happen if you don't finish your task today, this week, or this month? What will be the direct consequences?

Often, we procrastinate because we can afford to do so (or believe we can). The more time we have, the more likely we are to take our time over a task.

How many writers would complete their book if they didn't have a specific deadline from their editor? How many students would finish their papers without a submission date? How many projects would be left incomplete if there wasn't a hard deadline?

The other day, I was talking with a Pakistani who is studying for his Ph.D. in a Swedish university. He told me that in Sweden, students have very few constraints. They often have no clear deadline within which they're expected to complete their thesis. As a result, it's not rare for them to take many years to do so. Some students even decide to change topics after a couple of years because they no longer enjoy working on their current research topic. While I understand the value of having the freedom to study without external pressure, I believe that for many students, the lack of firm deadlines is counterproductive.

My point is that some people procrastinate because they don't have a sense of urgency pushing them to complete the job. Consequently, if you find yourself procrastinating, ask yourself whether you have a specific and immutable deadline. Then, assess what the consequences are if you fail to meet it. To create more urgency, you can take one or more of the following actions:

- Set a clear deadline. Choose a specific date that sounds realistic while still being somewhat challenging. This will create a sense of urgency.
- Install an accountability system. For instance, you can hire a coach or work with an accountability partner.
- Divide your projects into multiple milestones. This will make it less daunting. When Stephen King was asked how he writes, he replied, "One word at a time." Similarly, the Great Wall of China was built one stone at a time.
- Measure your progress often. See how you fare in regard to your milestones. Are you behind? If so, what can you do to catch up? As the management consultant, Peter Drucker said, "What gets measured gets done."

F. Lack of effective routines

Do you have a specific daily routine? If not, it may be the reason you end up procrastinating more than you'd like to.

As much as we like to fantasize about being able to do whatever we want, whenever we want, in truth, we're largely creatures of habit. As I'm writing this, I have almost complete freedom. I don't have a boss. I can work whenever and wherever I choose to. If I wanted to, I could even choose to stop working for weeks or months on end. Yet, I realize that such "freedom" can be a trap. Unlimited freedom doesn't make us happy. Without structure, sooner or later, we end up slacking off. We stop challenging ourselves and we cease to grow. As a result, we risk losing all meaning in our lives.

The bottom line is that, when it comes to living a meaningful and fulfilling life, routines are essential. Routines help you tackle your most important tasks every day. Thus, if you find yourself procrastinating, make sure you have a simple routine that prepares you for work each day. Don't worry though. Your routine doesn't have to be complicated. It can be very simple. For instance, it could be as simple as taking a few deep breaths and clearing your desk. Or it could be drinking tea and listening to a specific song.

The key is to get started. If you're able to remain focused on your task just for five or ten minutes, you'll likely keep working on it much longer. And the more you practice doing the same thing each day, the easier and more automatic the whole process will become.

To sum up, put in a place a simple routine by:

- Stacking together a few simple habits that calm your mind and prepare you for work,
- Repeating these habits every day, and
- Forgetting about motivation and simply starting work.

In **Part V. Developing Extraordinary Focus**, we'll cover in greater depth how to create a simple daily routine that will enhance your productivity.

G. Unnecessary friction

Your environment has a direct impact on your level of productivity. When well-optimized, it will enhance your productivity, but when poorly designed, it will lead to procrastination. As a general rule of thumb:

The easier it is to engage in productive behaviors, the more likely you are to do so—and vice versa. Consequently, when you optimize your environment you should focus on:

- Adding friction that make it harder to engage in unproductive behaviors or to develop bad habits, and
- Eliminating frictions to make it easier to engage in desirable behaviors or habits.

This works well because humans are fundamentally lazy. That is, each additional step dramatically reduces the likelihood of us actually doing something productive. Therefore:

- If you can't stop checking your phone, turn it off or put it in a different room.
- If you can't stop going on Facebook, block it using an app such as *Anti-social*.
- If you waste time on the internet, disconnect your Wi-Fi or even put your internet modem in your storage room (which is what I did when writing my previous book).

Remember, each step you add to an action creates friction and reduces the likelihood you'll perform it. For instance, just removing the finger identification on my phone reduced the number of times I checked it (I now have to enter my passcode each time). Moving the Gmail icon into a hidden folder on page three of my phone had a similar effect.

Similarly, for desirable behaviors, the more you can reduce friction, the better. For instance:

- If you want to work on a specific project on your computer, make the relevant files and folder(s) as easy to access as possible.
- If you want to go for a run in the morning, prepare your running gear the night before so that you're ready to go first thing.
- If you created a 90-day plan and want to stick to it, put the schedule on your desk or on your wall so that you can see it every day without having to exert any effort.

H. Mental overload

Do you feel overwhelmed, not knowing what to do anymore? Do you feel stuck and unable to get yourself to do anything?

Another reason you may procrastinate is simply that your mind is overwhelmed. You may have too much unfinished business taking up mental space, such as incomplete projects, unpaid taxes or unanswered emails. Your mind responds to these open loops by shutting down.

If you feel stuck, try the following:

- Take a sheet of paper and write down any tasks that you need to complete.
- Block time to complete as many of these tasks as possible. Start with the simplest one and work your way up. Or tackle the major task you've been putting off and finish it one hundred percent. This will generate incredible momentum and encourage you to accomplish even more tasks.

I hope that by now, you have a solid understanding of what procrastination is and how it works. Sure, you'll still procrastinate, but once you understand how it works and put in place the right workaround strategies and habits, you'll dramatically improve your chances of making an early start on any given day.

Remember, today is always the most important day of your life. Procrastinating is ignoring that reality and making tomorrow seem more appealing. Practice making good use of today and life will take care of itself.

* * *

Action step

Using your action guide, reflect on the reasons you may procrastinate. To do so, complete the following exercises:

1. Rate yourself on a scale from 1 to 10 (one being false, ten being true) for each statement below:

- I lack clarity regarding what I need to do or how to do it.
- I wait for motivation to arrive.
- I'm distracted unable to complete hard tasks.
- I'm afraid of not doing a good enough job.
- I have no clear deadline or sense of urgency.
- I have no daily routine to help me start work.
- My environment encourages unproductive or toxic behaviors.
- I have too many things to do, and I feel stuck.

2. Select one task you've been procrastinating on recently.

3. Write down the specific reason(s) you're procrastinating on this particular task (lack of clarity, insufficient awareness, poor focus, et cetera).

4. Write down one specific thing you could do to start that task.

PART II

UPDATING YOUR PERCEPTION OF TIME

Your perception of time has a major impact on the way you use it. Once you begin to perceive your time in a new, more empowering way, you'll find yourself being much more productive.

In this part, we'll discuss how to change the way you perceive your time so that you can make the most of it. It starts by using your past, present and future well.

1

USING PAST AND FUTURE PROPERLY

In truth, there is no such thing as time. The fact is you always live in the present moment. Whenever you travel back to the past or project yourself into the future, you do so in the present (but you can only do so in your mind). To put it another way, while the present moment is real, the past and the future are simply mental models we utilize to maximize the use of our "time" in the present and create a better "future" for ourselves.

Why does this matter? Because we tend to misuse or misunderstand these mental models, which not only creates suffering but also severely impacts our productivity.

Let's see how you might be using your past and your future in a disempowering way and what you can do instead.

A. Using your past effectively

Your past is nothing more than memories you recall in the present moment. In short, your past doesn't really exist (anymore). Yet, for many of us, it keeps controlling and limiting us in many ways. Here are some ways you may misuse the past:

- You feel sorry about yourself for what happened in the past.

- You waste tons of energy trying to change things from the past.
- You feel ashamed or guilty for what you did in the past.
- You idealize your past.

However, the past is not supposed to be a life sentence but a life lesson. Your past doesn't predict your future unless you allow it to. To use it well you must learn lessons and gather key insights that will empower yourself in the present moment and, hence, create a better future.

Now, there is nothing wrong with mentally traveling to the past. However, make sure you do so as a means to improve your present reality, not as a means to put yourself down. More specifically, I invite you to:

- Focus on all the things you did well. Remember all your successes and accomplishments, including small ones. Use them as fuel for your current goals.
- Remember times when you had courage. Remind yourself of things you did in spite of being afraid. Recall the things that you thought were challenging or even impossible for you, but you did them anyway. Then, feel a sense of pride.
- Give empowering meaning to negative events. Instead of dwelling on negative events from the past, give them an empowering meaning. For instance, you can do so by asking yourself questions like: What did you learn from them? In what ways did they help you to grow? Keep finding the positive in apparently negative experiences.
- Be self-compassionate. Understand that you didn't know any better at the time. If you had known better, you would have acted differently. Self-compassion acts as a safety net for your mental well-being. It may sound paradoxical but when you learn to become kinder to yourself, you'll accomplish more in the long term, and you will feel better.
- Practice letting go of difficult events. Do you keep reflecting

on the same events? If so, practice forgiving yourself and others, and then let go.

- See your past as detached from your present. Instead of letting the weight of your past drag you down, accept that it's over. To do so, visualize your past as a ball and chain that prevents you from moving freely. Then, picture yourself breaking free from your shackles. Experience the feeling of living in a present, untainted by the weight of your past. Repeat this exercise whenever needed.

If you want to learn how to replace your story with a more empowering one, you can refer to Book 4 in the *Mastery Series*, *Master Your Destiny*.

* * *

Action step

Using your action guide, write down the specific ways you may be misusing your past. Then, write down what you could focus on instead (remembering time you had courage, focusing on your accomplishments, et cetera).

B. Using your future effectively

As with every other human being, you were given the wonderful gift of imagination.

But how exactly should you use this gift?

Do so by projecting yourself into the future you wish to create and reverse engineering what actions you need to take now in order to build it. In other words, you can use this gift by planning for your future.

Planning enables you to identify what needs to be done while letting go of everything else you *could* be doing during that time. This eliminates distractions and establishes a clear path to follow. Projecting yourself into the future also enables you to anticipate problems and create a contingency plan to address them as they arise.

Once you've finished planning, you can project yourself into the future to experience the excitement of achieving your vision. Doing this will give you a renewed sense of motivation that will help you carry out the required work in the present.

Unfortunately, rather than using their imagination to create an effective plan, most people waste a great deal of energy worrying about the future. Avoid doing this since it is a misuse of your imagination. For instance, you may currently be misusing the future by:

- Worrying about a future event that hasn't happened yet,
- Focusing on all the things that could go wrong, and
- Making future events into a much bigger deal than they really are.

Instead, to make better use of your imagination and your future, I encourage you to:

- Visualize your goals and get excited about them. When you picture yourself having already achieved your goals, you create a powerful sense of excitement that you can use to determine your actions in the present.
- Imagine future events going as you have already planned them. Think of all the ways things can go well in the future.
- Identify all the things that could go wrong. By preparing yourself mentally for the worst, you can put in place a contingency plan to help you deal with future obstacles. Therefore, visualize the worst-case scenarios and imagine yourself dealing with them.
- Avoid making future events a bigger deal than they probably are. If you find yourself constantly stressing over an upcoming event, prepare as much as possible in the present (if you can). This will alleviate your anxiety. Alternatively, stick to your daily routine and practice immersing yourself

in the present moment each day. Also, consider writing down your worries and what you can do about them.

Remember, your imagination is a tool you can use to help you make the most of the present moment. Everything not serving that purpose is a misuse of your ability to "time-travel". Notice whenever you're misusing this magical ability and make changes accordingly.

* * *

Action step

Using your action guide, write down a few ways you're misusing your future.

Then, spend a few minutes visualizing yourself achieving your most exciting goals.

C. Using your present effectively

The present moment is the only thing you'll ever have. Whatever you do, think or feel, it happens in the present—in the "now".

The "now" is where the magic happens. It's where you have fun, do meaningful work and create deeper connections with the people around you. The more you understand and value the *present moment*, the better your life will become.

When you're lost in your thoughts, dwelling on the past or worrying about the future, you let the depth and importance of the present moment slip through your fingers. You live in an illusory world, moving away from the reality in front of you. You escape your responsibility and let time slip away—time that you will never be able to get back.

However, it doesn't have to be that way.

You can learn to immerse yourself in the depths of the present moment and use it to work toward being and acting as the person you aspire to be. To do so, you must practice taking each day seriously. Ultimately, one day is a small unit of life—it is a "micro-life". When you have a miserable day, you have a miserable "micro-life". Repeat this process long enough and you end up far away from the life you intended to create.

Your day is too precious to let it pass without setting clear intentions for it. Now, don't get me wrong, I'm not telling you that you need to be productive every single minute of every single day. But I am suggesting you should become more intentional in the way you spend it. How? By assessing whether the activities you engage in during your day are meaningful, challenging, memorable, enjoyable, self-worth enhancing, effective, and/or health-enhancing.

We'll discuss in greater depth these seven criteria in **Part III. Making a Meaningful Use of Your Time.**

When you see each day as a micro-life, you suddenly have many lives, and this gives you many opportunities to start over. Here is a great question to ask yourself:

If I keep doing what I'm doing today, will I end up where I want to be five years from now?

Will I look back at these past five years and think, "Wow that was amazing! That was meaningful and well worth it". Or will I think, "Where did those five years go?"

To make each day more memorable, take a moment in the morning to acknowledge the day ahead of you. See it for what it is: life itself—not just another day. Just because it's only a tiny fragment of your life doesn't change its essence. It's made of life itself. To paraphrase Steve Jobs, you should practice treating each day as your last, because, without a doubt, one day you will wake up and it *will* be your last day.

Now, let's look at a few concrete habits you can adopt to seize the day and value it as much as you should.

a. Be grateful for today

When you wake up each morning, acknowledge the day ahead of you. Thank the universe for granting you a new day. Starting your day by expressing your gratitude is an excellent way to begin your new (micro)life.

As the researcher, Robert Emmon, wrote in *The Little Book of Gratitude*:

"Living gratefully begins with affirming the good and recognizing its sources. It is the understanding that life owes me nothing and all the good I have is a gift, accompanied by an awareness that nothing can be taken for granted."

Gratitude grounds you in the present moment and makes you realize all the wonderful things you already have in your life. It is particularly useful if you're continuously trying to escape the present by living in the future. Such behavior creates a state of continuous lack and chronic dissatisfaction, which is neither an effective nor a satisfying way to use your time. Gratitude acts as an antidote to such negativity.

Studies have shown that gratitude comes with a plethora of benefits, as underlined by Robert Emmon:

- Keeping a gratitude diary for two weeks reduces stress by twenty-eight percent and depression by sixteen percent in healthcare practitioners.
- Gratitude is related to twenty-three percent lower levels of stress hormones.
- Writing a letter of gratitude reduced feelings of hopelessness in eighty-eight percent of suicidal patients and increased levels of optimism in ninety-four percent of them.

Being grateful for each new day might seem too simplistic or even meaningless. However, if you do not stop to acknowledge the day ahead of you, your days will start blending together and you'll start behaving as if the upcoming day didn't matter. You'll say things like, "I'll do it tomorrow". Being less deliberate, you'll tend to succumb to toxic behaviors that fail to support the ideal life you seek to create.

Below are some prompts you can use to acknowledge your day:

- Thank you for this new day. I'll make the most of it.
- Today is a new opportunity to start afresh and let go of everything from the past.
- Today could very well be my last day. I'll act as if I hold my entire life in my hands.
- I'll make the most of today. By doing so, I know I'm building the best life possible.
- Today is always the most important day of my life, because it's the only day I have control over.

What about you? Are you practicing gratitude on a daily basis? If not, what could you start doing every day to cultivate more gratitude in your life?

b. Plan your day

Once you've acknowledged the gift of today, you need to spend time thinking of the best way to unwrap it. You can do so by planning the activities you want to focus on. Planning your day is a sign you value it—the same way you plan your wedding because you value the relationship with your soon-to-be spouse. As a rule of thumb, the more deliberate you are with your day and time, the happier and more productive you will be.

To plan your day, you can simply take a pen and paper and write down the few things you want to focus on that day. Ask yourself:

- What would make today a good day?
- What would make today memorable?
- What would move me closer to my ideal vision?

The key is to make sure you work on your most valuable task and complete it. Without doubt, this is one of the biggest "secrets" to high productivity. In **Part V. Develop Extraordinary Focus,** we'll discuss in greater depth how to do this. Consequently, schedule your most important task for first thing in the morning. Or, if this is not possible, set aside time later during the day to work on it. Make the task your priority. Make it what you absolutely *must* accomplish during the micro-life that constitutes today.

As you write down your tasks for the day, I also encourage you to write the date (day, month, year, and day of the week). While you do so, remind yourself that today really matters. Pause for just a couple of seconds to let the day's importance and wonder sink in.

The bottom line is, planning your day increases the value of your time by forcing you to be more intentional. Keep planning every day consistently, week after week, month after month, and your productivity will skyrocket.

c. Fulfill your duty

Once you have set your daily tasks, focus on the first job until you complete it one hundred percent. Then, repeat the process for the next task and the next. The following technique will help:

Create mental separation between the person who plans and the one who actually executes the plan. When you plan, see yourself as the CEO of your day. When you work on your tasks, see yourself as the employee doing their work.

As an employee, all you have to do is to tackle the tasks, one at a time, without overthinking them. You merely have to trust the CEO's ability to plan the days efficiently, knowing that, over the long term, the company (you) will achieve the results you're after.

The main benefits of this mental separation of roles are that, for the most part, you can:

- Remove motivation from the equation,
- Eliminate indecision, and
- Reduce confusion.

We'll discuss this mental model in greater depth in **Part V** of this book.

d. Slow down time

What if I told you that, like Neo in the movie "The Matrix", you could slow down time?

Sorry, I'm afraid you can't.

You might not actually be able to slow down time, but you can relax your mind. As you do so, you'll feel as though you have more time and better control over your actions. To relax your mind, you can meditate, use breathing techniques or practice awareness exercises.

Such exercises will help you slow your mind and delve deeper into the present moment. By doing so, you'll notice that your tendency to engage in negative thinking or to travel into the past or the future mentally will decrease. While unpleasant thoughts might arise, their pulling power will be reduced, and you'll be able to let them go more easily. The present moment will become more intense while your ability to focus will dramatically increase. In short, you'll be anchored in reality while your unpleasant thoughts will recede into the distance and become more and more unreal.

This is the power of slowing down time. You'll find that the more you can return to the present moment, the more in control you will feel. In such a state of presence, you'll accomplish more while feeling as though you're doing less. That's the paradox of such a state of mind.

For instance, when I wrote my book *Master Your Emotions*, I would often alternate between writing and meditation sessions. I would write for an hour or so and then meditate for fifteen to twenty minutes. When I returned to writing, my mind would be relaxed and few negative thoughts would arise.

In his book *The Practicing Mind*, Thomas M. Sterner relates an interesting experiment. During a busy day in which he had to prepare two pianos before a concert, he decided to put all his effort into "deliberately working slowly".

As he recalled:

"Working this way might sound counterproductive, but I had been putting way too many hours on the career end of my life's equation, and I was out of balance. I was tired and frustrated. I couldn't get a day off, so going slowly for at least one day seemed rather appealing to me."

He was shocked when he looked at the clock at the end of the day:

"When I got into the truck, its clock radio came on with the turn of my key, and I was dumbfounded. So little time had passed compared to what I had usually spent on the same job in the past that I was sure the clock was incorrect [...] I had cut over forty percent off the usual time."

The point is, when you act slowly and in a more deliberate way, you waste less energy and slow down your mind, which allows you to become more effective. As a result, you often end up working faster, while experiencing significantly less stress.

One thing I've always found surprising is how calm and in control experts in their field seem to be. You seldom see a CEO running to his office even when an important job is waiting. Nor do you see a martial arts expert or a world-class musician being in a hurry before a performance. Most highly successful people are focused. They understand that they must control their mind and focus their attention on the task in front of them. By doing so, they're able to "slow down" time and act effectively in any situation.

What about you? Are you able to slow down time during your day, or does it always feel as though you're in a rush?

To slow down time, I encourage you to meditate for a few minutes before starting a task. I also invite you to take regular breaks to reinstate that condition by meditating, performing breathing exercises or listening to soothing music. Finally, when you work, practice moving slowly and deliberately.

Here are some simple exercises you can try:

Awareness exercise

- Isolate one sense and practice focusing on it for a moment (start with hearing for instance). Try to hear things you've never noticed before.
- Next, move your attention to another sense and do the same.
- Repeat this exercise for each sense (touch, sight, hearing, smell and taste).
- Finally, try to be aware of all your senses at the same time.

This simple exercise will ground you and help you to feel more present and calmer.

Breathing exercises

Breath slowly, using the following frequency as mentioned by Gurucharan Singh Khalsa, Ph.D., and Yogi Bhajan, Ph.D., in their book, *Breathwalk*:

- Eight cycles per minute (offers relief from stress and increased mental awareness).
- Four cycles per minute (produces positive shifts in mental

function, intense feelings of awareness, increased visual clarity and heightened bodily sensitivity).

Meditating exercise

Try this exercise as recommended by Brendon Burchard in *High Performance Habits*. A couple of minutes might be enough.

"Repeat the word 'release' in your mind over and over. As you do, command your body to release all the tension in your shoulders, in your neck, in your face and jaw. Release the tension in your back and your legs. Release the tension in your mind and spirit. If this is hard, just focus on each part of your body, breathe deeply, and repeat the word 'release' in your mind."

* * *

Action step

Complete the following exercises in your action guide.

- Write down one thing you could do every day to express your gratitude.
- Write down the date each morning and take a few seconds to acknowledge your day (using the prompts described earlier).
- Practice completing your key tasks through to the end.
- Try awareness, meditation and/or breathing exercises to calm your mind before working on your designated tasks.

2

PERCEIVING TIME AS AN INVESTMENT

Most people spend their time but fail to invest it effectively.

The wonderful thing with time is that we can only live in the present. We cannot consume tomorrow or the next five years in advance. In other words, although we can live beyond our means financially, we can never live beyond the present moment.

Unfortunately, the drawback to this is that we can never store our time or our energy. Whenever we fail to use the energy we have today, it is forever gone.

Now, what's the difference between spending time and investing it?

When you *spend* time, you waste it by doing things that fail to bring any tangible long-term benefits. For instance, spending your time could mean binge-watching Netflix, mindlessly scrolling through your Facebook newsfeed or playing video games for hours on end. By engaging in such unproductive activities, you are "leaking" energy. In other words, the energy you have at your disposal during this period simply dissipates—*and that energy can never be recovered*. A chunk of your life will have disappeared, just like that. Poof.

Unfortunately, you cannot build a better future and create a deeper sense of fulfillment by indulging in instant gratification or engaging in unproductive activities. Time spent in this manner simply cannot be invested to reap future dividends.

Conversely, when you *invest* your time, you will utilize all your available energy and transform it into something valuable. For instance, you can transform your energy into:

- Memories that will stay with you for the rest of your life,
- Skills that will serve you for years to come,
- Knowledge that will make you wiser and improve your life,
- Products or services that will allow you to express your creativity and serve others, and/or
- Mental/physical well-being that enables you to maintain and increase your overall energy levels.

By investing your time wisely every day, you'll build a better future. Therefore, I encourage you to assess how effectively you're using your time right now. Don't get me wrong though. I'm not saying you should never watch a TV series or spend time on social media. You also need to rest, but you usually need significantly less down time than you realize. And there are often better alternatives. For instance, you might find that playing board games with your friends or reading a good book is all the relaxation you need.

Personally, I've found that studying languages or taking online classes is less tiring and more enjoyable than I expected. Some of these activities can even reinvigorate me. As Arnold Bennet wrote in, *How to Live on 24 Hours a Day*:

"One of the chief things which my typical man has to learn is that the mental faculties are capable of a continuous hard activity; they do not tire like an arm or a leg. All they want is change—not rest, except in sleep."

So, even if you feel tired, you might have more energy left than you expect. In fact, the US Navy Seal, David Goggins, author of *Can't Hurt Me*, argues that when our mind is telling us we're exhausted, we're really only forty percent empty. This is what he calls "the forty percent rule". This rule may or may not be accurate. However, it is certainly true that we can often do more than we think, both mentally *and* physically.

What about you? Do you invest your time to build a better future? Do you challenge yourself to do more enjoyable or meaningful things during your day? Or do you spend your time on trivial activities that bring you no long-term benefit?

If you spend most of your evenings glued to the TV or to your computer, ask yourself whether this is really how you want to be using one of the scarcest resources on earth.

The bottom line is, if you don't invest your time well, it will be gone forever. If you don't respect the day ahead, it will slip through your fingers and be wasted. So, learn to invest your time effectively. Create wonderful memories, develop invaluable skills, acquire insightful knowledge, build amazing products or services and stay in shape mentally and physically. And don't forget to have fun in the process!

Understanding the Law of Diminishing Returns

A key concept to grasp when it comes to using your time well is the *Law of Diminishing Returns*. According to this law, more isn't always better. There is a point where more of something doesn't add anything to your life. For instance, let's say you binge-watched a TV series for four hours. Now, how would you measure the level of enjoyment you received from watching it for four hours as opposed to one hour. Did you get four times more enjoyment? Twice as much enjoyment? The same amount of enjoyment? Tricky, isn't it?

At what point can you say that you hit the *Law of Diminishing Returns*? I don't have the answer. However, it's likely to be less than four hours. If so, you would probably be better off watching the series for one hour and doing something else with the rest of your time.

Here's my point. You can *invest* the energy you have each day in designing a better life, or you can let it dissipate forever. However, today's energy can never be used tomorrow, so invest your time wisely. It will soon be gone.

Investment vs. spending ratio

How much of your time is invested vs. spent each day? I encourage you to take a closer look at this ratio. Ask yourself:

"If I keep the same ratio moving forward, will I be able to do most of the things I want? Will I look back at my life and feel as though it was worth it? If not, how could I start investing my time more wisely?"

Let's use a concrete example to help you understand why adjusting this ratio just a little can be so powerful over the long term.

Let's say you watch TV two hours per day and consider it an unproductive use of your time (i.e., it is time spent). Now, extrapolate how much time you would have spent on the same activity over a longer period of time. This would be:

- 14 hours per week,
- 62 hours per month,
- 730 hours per year,
- 7,300 hours per decade, and
- 21,900 hours over three decades.

21,900 hours is the equivalent of watching TV for 16 hours a day, for 3.75 years! Just imagine what you could accomplish if you invested that extra 21,900 hours wisely.

Now, let's err on the side of caution and assume you can only cut the time you spend in front of the TV in half. Over three decades you could still reclaim more than 10,000 hours of your time. That's not bad, is it?

Once you've completed this exercise, think about all the exciting things you want to do before you die. Perhaps you want to travel all around the world. Perhaps you want to learn Japanese. Perhaps you want to set up a charity.

Whatever dreams you may have, they are, in most cases, within your reach. The more excited you are about them—and the more clearly you can visualize them—the more compelled you'll be to take action to close the gap between where you are and where you want to be.

* * *

Action step

Review your typical week and complete the following exercises using your action guide:

- Write down one daily activity you would rate as being a poor use of your time (as opposed to being an investment).
- Calculate the total number of hours you'll have spent on this activity over a lifetime (extrapolate assuming you'll live until 75).
- Write down the most exciting thing you could be doing instead. Don't limit yourself and write what you really, really want to do.
- Feel the pain and regret you'll experience from not having achieved this goal.
- Now, visualize yourself having achieved it. Get excited about it!
- Finally, visualize how much progress you could make toward that exciting goal in the next year or the next decade if you free up the time by removing that single unproductive activity.

3

UNDERSTANDING COMPOUND EFFECT AND LONG-TERM THINKING

How often do you consider where you want to be next year, in five years or even ten years from now?

Studies have shown that the ability to think long term is one of the best predictors of success. People who regularly focus on where they want to be in the future, make better decisions in the present. They tend to eat healthier food, be more productive at work and save and invest more money than others. In his book *Goals!* success expert, Brian Tracy, wrote:

"Dr. Edward Banfield of Harvard University concluded, after more than fifty years of research, that 'long-time perspective' was the most important determinant of financial and personal success in life. Banfield defined long-time as the 'ability to think several years into the future while making decisions in the present.'"

Unfortunately, we aren't born as long-term thinkers. If anything, we are designed to focus on the short term as part of our survival mechanism, but we can learn. One way to do so is by creating a long-term plan and continuously visualizing where we want to be in the future. As we continually picture our idea future, we increase our odds of reaching it. By focusing every day on where we want to be years from now, we'll inevitably make progress toward our goal.

The key is to understand the power of consistency and how it accumulates over the weeks, months and years. As human beings, we tend to think linearly. We struggle to grasp the exponential results that daily actions can bring when sustained over the long term. Yet, daily actions are insanely powerful. When performed over a long period of time, they activate the power of accumulation based on the following simple truth:

What brings positive changes isn't what we do every *other* day but what we do *every* day.

For instance, if you study a foreign language every day for long enough, you will inevitably make noticeable progress. Each day will build on the previous one, allowing you to improve your skills. On the other hand, if you only study once a week, the time spent doing so will be fairly ineffective. Why? Because you will fail to set the accumulative effect into motion. You won't build momentum and you certainly won't see any exponential results. If anything, you'll keep forgetting what you learned previously and will have to revisit the same material over and over.

For this reason, one unit of time is much more valuable when part of a daily routine than when taken in isolation. Therefore, if you wish to achieve exponential results, learn to leverage the power of consistency. This is what I did with my online business. For the past five years, I have worked on it almost every day, which has enabled me to generate momentum and activate the power of accumulation. As a result, I was able to achieve a great deal.

What about you? What daily habits could you implement to turbocharge each unit of your time?

Here are some examples of the power of daily consistency:

- If you write just 500 words every day you will have written five books like this one in just one year. In ten years, you'll have written fifty books. And in forty years, you'll have produced an astonishing 200 books! Of course, there is more to producing a book than just writing. You must also conduct research, develop an outline, create a cover and so on. But I'm sure you get my point.

- If you learn just five words of a foreign language every day, you'll have learned 1,825 words in a year, and 9,125 words over five years. That's enough to be fluent in any language!
- If you walk just two miles each day, you'll have walked over 700 miles in a year. Over forty years, you'll have walked over 29,000 miles, which is more than walking the circumference of the earth (which is around 24,901 miles).

The point is this. Each unit of time is not made equal. When you use the power of daily consistency, you put more energy into each unit of time and set the accumulative effect into motion. Over the long run, this can lead to exponential results that will often exceed your wildest expectations.

The power of long-term thinking

Now, thinking long term is not easy. Rather than delaying their personal gratification, most people want things immediately. And this actually makes sense considering the present is more valuable than the uncertain future.

However, visualizing a compelling future can also drive you to act in the present with a higher level of excitement. In fact, some studies have shown that people often derive more pleasure from anticipating a future event than from the event itself. Remember your last vacation. You probably enjoyed planning your trip weeks, if not months, ahead of time. You already saw yourself relaxing on the beach. You imagined yourself having fun with your family or friends. Or you visualized yourself exploring a new city, feeling totally free and relaxed.

The point is, thinking long term is much easier when you have an exciting vision you can't wait to turn into reality. Under these conditions, the present moment becomes an opportunity to move toward that vision. Each small step moves you closer to your goal and becomes a reason to rejoice and celebrate.

In short, by projecting yourself into the future, you can bring the joy forward and use it as fuel in the present. And when you have a clear and compelling enough vision that you work toward consistently, there is almost nothing you cannot achieve.

Enjoying the process

Thinking long term becomes more powerful when you learn to derive pleasure from making daily progress toward your goal. When the journey is pleasant, the destination becomes less relevant. And, paradoxically, you become much more likely to reach it.

While many people receive a kick from instant gratification, long-term thinkers are different. They always keep an eye on their goals and learn to enjoy the process that will help attain them. Generating excitement from within, long-term thinkers take great pleasure when accumulating small daily wins. Eager to make progress, they never stop projecting themselves into the future, knowing they're moving closer to their dreams each day. Slow and steady progress becomes the yardstick they use to measure their progress.

The bottom line is, if you spend time thinking of your long-term vision every day, you'll inevitably achieve more than you otherwise would.

For instance, I often visualize myself accomplishing my goals. I see myself writing all the books I've planned to write this year and can't help but feel excited about being so productive. I'm also hopeful they'll reach a large audience and will be useful to as many readers as possible. While I do procrastinate—sometimes more than I'd like to —I'm eager to make progress each and every day. I just know that if I continue to do so, the future will be bright. As I like to repeat to myself:

"Do the work and you can have anything you desire in your life."

What about you? Are you deriving pleasure from moving closer to your goals, or are you succumbing to instant gratification and procrastinating over the things that really matter to you?

When the excitement of making daily progress becomes stronger than the pleasure you receive from instant gratification, your ability to achieve long-term goals will increase dramatically. Consequently, you should work on shifting the balance by envisioning all the wonderful things you're about to create. Then, go back to work.

* * *

Action step

Complete the following exercises in your action guide:

- Write down the one daily habit that would have the biggest impact on your productivity long term if you were to implement it. Imagine what the impact would be if you stuck to it for the next five to ten years. (Whatever you imagine, the impact will probably be far greater due to the power of accumulation.)
- Practice visualizing your long-term goals for a few minutes every day.
- Develop the habit of acknowledging your small daily wins. Write down what you could do to celebrate your wins. For instance, you could draw a circle on a calendar each day you complete each task that relates to your main goals.

4

CREATING URGENCY

Do you keep wasting time on trivial things, acting as though you will live forever?

Time is the essence of life. If you feel as though you have an infinite amount of time, you risk wasting it instead of investing it in meaningful activities.

Creating a sense of urgency is another tool you can use to transform your relationship with time. To generate urgency, first, you must stop thinking in terms of years. For instance, many people set yearly goals. You might say what's wrong with that? The problem is that one year is such a long time. It is almost impossible to stay motivated when you focus a goal that is one year away. It's just too far into the future to foster any action today. And because you can always start tomorrow, next week, or next month, you may end up procrastinating.

To increase the value of your time, you must stop giving yourself so much room to slack off. You must stop setting vague goals that are too far into the future to lead you to act in the present.

A. Think in ninety-day periods

A good way to tackle bigger goals is to chunk them down. But an even better way is to think in ninety-day units of time, as Brian P. Moran and Michael Lennington wrote in their book, *The 12 Weeks Year*. Ninety days is enough time to complete a significant project and make serious progress toward any major long-term goal. With ninety-day goals, you can almost see the finish line. As such, you will be incentivized to take immediate action and move quickly.

In short, as soon as you think in ninety-day periods, urgency starts kicking in. Imagine if you had to achieve your yearly goals within ninety days. What would you be doing? The answer is, you'll give much more value to your time. Failing to work on your goals for just one day would significantly reduce your chance of reaching them. Think about it this way:

If you were to turn your yearly goals into ninety-day goals, you would need to accomplish four days of work in just one day!

Of course, I'm not saying you could reach your annual goals in ninety days but imagine for a moment you had to. How much more value would you place on your time?

B. Implement frequent deadlines

Another way to create a sense of urgency is to implement frequent deadlines. As Parkinson's Law states, "work expands so as to fill in the time available for its completion." Without enough milestones along the way, you'll find yourself tackling your tasks at the last minute. This is what many students do when given school papers.

By breaking down your goals into multiple milestones, you can not only create a sense of urgency but you can also track your progress more effectively. In addition, each time you reach a milestone, it gives you a hit of dopamine, helping you stay motivated along the way.

The great news is that almost any goal can be broken down into smaller goals. By reaching each of these sub-goals, you'll make steady progress and will eventually hit your major long-term goal. As the saying goes, the best way to eat an elephant is one bite at a time.

For instance, when writing books, I find milestones to be extremely effective. Without specific deadlines and milestones along the way, I would probably never complete my books. Without a sense of urgency, I would end up creating numerous excuses to do anything but write. Instead of writing, I would tweak sentences, rearrange paragraphs and take numerous and interminable little "breaks".

Therefore, to ensure I complete my books, I first set a deadline. Then, I establish a few milestones, such as completing the outline and finishing the first draft. Finally, I tell my editor when I'll send him the manuscript. Of course, this process is not perfect, and I don't always meet my deadlines, but creating milestones within a defined work schedule helps me tremendously.

Note that I'm fairly disciplined and self-motivated. If you're not, you might need to implement additional milestones and create a stronger accountability system by hiring a coach or by teaming up with an accountability partner.

To sum up, adding milestones creates a sense of urgency and gives you clarity in terms of what needs to be done each day. As a result, you'll use each unit of your time much more effectively.

Action step

- As a thought experiment, imagine you had only ninety days to achieve what you usually do in one full year. Feel the sense of urgency this creates and imagine how much more you'll achieve with such a mindset.
- Now, choose one long-term goal and write it down in your action guide.
- Break it down into a few ninety-day goals. Make sure it is a tangible goal you can picture. Make it a little challenging (to create urgency).
- Add specific milestones by setting monthly and weekly goals.

- Finally, write down what you need to do today to start making progress toward those goals.

Now, let's see in greater depth how you can use your time more effectively. In the next part, you'll discover seven criteria you can use to assess how effectively you're using your time. Exciting, isn't it?

PART III

MAKING A MEANINGFUL USE OF YOUR TIME

To become a master of your time you must learn how to use it meaningfully. But what does this mean, and what criteria should you take into account to accomplish it?

In this section, we'll introduce a simple framework to ensure you're using your time in a satisfying way. But before we do this, let's destroy the biggest myth that may prevent you from making the most of your time.

1

THE FIVE MOST DANGEROUS WORDS
YOU MUST STOP USING

How often do you say the following words:

"I don't have time"?

These days everybody seems to be busy. In many aspects, being busy has become a badge of honor. I lived in Japan for many years and people always seem to be busy there. Being idle is probably perceived as rude. Idleness means you're not a productive member of society. At least, that's how the Japanese might interpret idleness.

Now, why are we so busy, and why do we keep saying we don't have time? I believe there are a few reasons for this:

- **We refuse to take responsibility for our lives.** Saying we don't have enough time gets us off the hook. It gives us valid reasons to avoid making difficult changes to our lives. We don't have to rethink the way we work, go to bed early or replace toxic activities with more productive ones.
- **We want to position ourselves as victims.** By claiming we don't have time we invite our friends' commiseration. We can then pat each other on the back and strengthen our mutual beliefs that we're all so busy.

- **We lack the motivation to do something.** Saying we don't have time to do something is another way to say it's not really important to us. It could mean we need to make our goals more compelling.
- **We feel the need to look busy.** There is a cultural aspect that leads many people to act as though they are busy. Being busy is seen as cool. It means we're doing "stuff". Over time, such thinking can become a self-fulfilling prophecy and a collective illusion. As a result, people keep adding more and more stuff to their calendar instead of thinking more strategically and more constructively.

What about you? Do you recognize yourself in any of the above?

You have more time than you think

But are we really that busy, and is there really nothing we can do to escape the never-ending rat race? In truth, you probably have more time than you think. Here is an interesting statistic given by Jean Paul Zogby, in his book *The Time Miracle*:

"On average the typical American will watch around 80,486 hours—or more than 9 years' worth of TV in a lifetime!"

He continued:

"The average American will spend around 5.3 years of their life glued online to a digital screen."

In short, most of us will spend over fourteen years of our lives watching TV, using the internet or being glued to our smartphones. But it gets worse. Once we subtract the eight hours needed for sleep each day, that number goes up to twenty-one years. That's over a quarter of our lifespan spent in front of a screen!

So, do you really think you don't have any spare time? If so, I urge you to rethink how you spend your day.

The point is, we all have the same twenty-four hours in every day. Some people use this time to achieve extraordinary things, never complaining about a lack of time. Others are always running around complaining they're "too busy". Yet, these same ever so busy people never seem to accomplish anything significant.

Be careful. Whenever you say, "I don't have time", you give your power away to circumstances around you, and you let external factors dictate your behavior instead of shaping it from within. This is due to a lack of priorities, which comes from having unclear values and poorly defined goals. Or as I like to put it:

Busyness is laziness in thinking (although I'm pretty sure I read that somewhere).

Being busy is the price you pay for failing to define what truly matters to you.

As the doctor, YouTuber and productivity nerd, Ali Abdaal, puts it:

"*Whenever you say,* 'I don't have time' *what you actually say is,* 'I choose not to make the time for this activity because it's not that important to me right now.'"

Here is the thing:

Nobody is putting a gun to your head, telling you what you should or shouldn't be doing. You *chose* to spend time on social media, watch TV or stay in your current job. If you truly want to achieve your goals, you must take complete responsibility for the way you use your time. Nobody else can do it for you. And taking control starts by knowing exactly what you want and what truly matters to *you*.

Therefore, stop saying, "I don't have time." Banish this sentence from your mind. Instead, replace it with more empowering statements such as:

"I choose not to make the time for that thing right now," or

"I have a lot of projects I'm focusing on right now so this will have to wait."

Then, when something is important to you, ask yourself:

- How can I make time to study?

- How can I make time to exercise?
- How can I make time to play with my kids?
- How can I make time to work on my side hustle?

Action step

Using your action guide, rate each statement below on a scale from 1 to 10 (one being false, ten being true):

- I don't take full responsibility for my time.
- I position myself as a victim, complaining I don't have time.
- I fail to work on my goals because my reason isn't compelling enough.
- I feel the need to look busy to fit in with others and avoid having to think more strategically.

Whenever you find yourself complaining you don't have time, do one of the following things:

- Say to yourself, "I choose not to make the time for this thing right now."
- Ask yourself, "How *can* I make the time for this thing?"

It will help you uncover your priorities.

If you feel you don't have time, it might also be because you're unaware of how much time you waste. If so, the exercise in the following section will be eye-opening.

2

KEEPING A TIME LOG

Self-awareness is the prerequisite to any major change. The more aware you are of the way you spend your time, the more you'll regain control over it and be able to redirect it toward more meaningful activities.

In this section, let's do a simple exercise that will shed light on how you use your time. To complete this exercise, write down in detail all your daily activities for the next seven days. Make sure you include everything you do before, during and after work. As you do so, you'll realize:

- How much time you actually work versus engage in unproductive activities such as tackling minor tasks, wasting time on social media or checking your emails compulsively.
- How you spend your time outside of work and whether it is what you really want to do. For instance, you may be watching TV or Netflix for hours while there are other, more constructive, things you could be doing.

We tend to believe we know how we spend our time, but we often don't. Therefore, make sure you complete this exercise, using the action guide.

By analyzing how you use your time each day, you begin to regain control over it. This new awareness fosters personal responsibility and enables you to increase the value you give to your time.

* * *

Action step

Using your action guide, complete the time log.

3

BEING PRODUCTIVE THE RIGHT WAY

As I mentioned in Book 3 in this series, *Master Your Focus*, to be truly productive, you must work on clarifying your long-term vision. We won't go into great depth on how to do that in this book, but if you want to learn more, refer to *Master Your Focus*.

The idea is simple:

What you focus on every day should be aligned with your long-term vision. Because, if it's not, you'll end up in a completely different place from where you intended. Although this sounds obvious, how many people work hard every day but fail to reflect on where they're actually trying to go?

A question I like to ask myself is:

"If I keep doing what I'm doing today/this week, will I end up where I want to be five or ten years from now?

If the answer is no, I know I'm going to have to make some adjustments.

If you have no clarity, you cannot allocate your time effectively. Neither can you use your ability to focus smartly. As a result, you end up "leaking" your precious energy each day—energy that you will never be able to recover. In short, the less clarity you have, the more energy you will waste during your day.

While it might take you a lot of thinking before you gain clarity, you can start the process now by trying to answer the questions listed below.

A. Fifteen key questions to help you gain clarity

a. Eliciting desire

1. What do I really, really want?

2. If I were to wake up tomorrow, completely alone without any family member, friend or colleague to influence my decisions, what would I do differently?

3. If I were to be totally honest with myself, what would I start doing now? What would I stop doing?

4. If I was guaranteed to succeed in everything I do, where would I want to be in five years?

5. If I could spend my day exactly the way I wanted to, what would my ideal day consist of?

6. If I could focus on doing only one thing for the rest of my life, what would it be?

7. If I understood and truly believed I could achieve absolutely anything I wanted to, by sticking to it for long enough, what would I pursue in the next three to five years?

b. Finding your strengths and unique abilities

8. When am I the happiest at work and what am I doing?

9. What do I find so easy to do I genuinely wonder why others struggle to do the same thing?

10. What do people around me say I'm great at?

c. Uncovering your passion

11. What did I enjoy doing when I was a kid?

12. Who do I envy and why?

13. If I had all the time and money in the world, what would I do with it?

14. If I had complete confidence and were already my absolute best self, what would I be doing with my life?

15. How do I want to express myself to the world?

B. Characteristics of a good vision

To ensure you're productive in a meaningful way, you must develop an exciting vision to chase every day. An exciting vision consists of the following components:

a. It's exciting to you (obviously). It may sound common sense, but you should really want that vision to become a reality. It should pull you with its intensity.

b. It's crystal clear. You have a clear picture in mind of how you will feel, where you will be and what you will be doing once you've reached that goal. However, bear in mind that developing a crystal-clear vision is difficult. You'll need many iterations before developing the correct one, but this is better than having no vision at all. Remember, you cannot reach a target that you don't set in the first place. A clear vision will enable you to reverse-engineer what you need to do and ensure you make progress each and every day.

c. It is aligned with your values. We all value different things. Your vision should be aligned with your core values. It should allow you to live by them every single day. Values are not abstract things you talk about during cocktail parties to look smart. They are things that directly influence the way you live your life and dictate most of your decisions.

For example, someone who values autonomy above anything else will make different choices at work or in their personal life than someone whose primary value is contribution or connection with others. Think of your values as being your philosophy or your way of life. Also, make sure that your values are yours, not values imposed on you by people around you or by society as a whole.

Finally, when you write down your top three values, define them as specifically as possible. For instance, let's say you value safety the most. If so, what exactly do you mean by safety?

Safety could mean:

- Working for the government or a major conglomerate with little or no risk of being made redundant,
- Living in a neighborhood where you can go out at any time of the day or night without fear for your safety, or
- Having the confidence in your ability to switch jobs or find a new job easily because of the experience and the skills you have developed over the years.

As you can see, the same values can mean different things to different people.

d. It allows you to feel alive and to express yourself the way you wish. Your vision should give you a framework within which you can express yourself in a meaningful way. That is, it should enable you to live by your core values but also to express your strengths and unique personality traits.

e. It pushes you to challenge yourself. Finally, your vision should also push you to challenge yourself and move beyond your comfort zone. This will allow you to feel alive and thrive instead of just surviving or going through the motions. The more you learn about yourself, the more powerful your vision will become, and the better results you will achieve in every area of your life. So, make sure you take time to build your vision and refine it over time. Having a great vision will ensure that you're making effective use of your time and, as a result, are truly productive.

* * *

Action step

- Using your action guide, answer the fifteen questions.
- Write down your vision (don't worry if it's still vague as you can refine it over time).

4

HOW TO USE YOUR TIME WELL

We all want to make the most of our time but how can we ensure we do so?

In this section, we'll review a few criteria to consider when deciding the best way to allocate your time. I believe time well spent should include one or more of the seven components below:

1) Meaningful:

- Does the thing I work on have meaning to me? Does it align with my values, personality or goals?
- Is the time I spend with this person or this group of people meaningful? Do I enjoy the conversation? Do I experience a sense of connection?
- Does what I do enable me to express my creativity? Does it nourish my soul? Does it make me come alive?

2) Enjoyable:

- Do I genuinely enjoy what I do?
- Is it fun? Does it make me smile or laugh?
- Does it help me relax?

3) Challenging:

- Is what I do challenging? Does it require me to move beyond my comfort zone and try things I've never tried before? Does it require me to stretch my current skills?
- Does it engage my creativity and my problem-solving skills?

4) Memorable:

- Does what I do create great memories I'll remember for years?
- Is it exciting or new?
- Is it playful or even somewhat silly?

5) Self-worth enhancing:

- Does it enhance my self-worth?
- Does it build my character and improve me as a person?

6) Effective (For work/study):

- Is it the most effective way to approach my task or work on my goals, or could I do it more effectively?

7) Health enhancing:

- Does it help me stay healthy or improve my health?

Now, let's look at specific examples to help you understand each criterion more deeply. For instance, just a few weeks ago I was watching Netflix for many hours each night. Now, was this a good use of my time? Well, let's find out using the criteria above.

Was it meaningful? No. No, I cannot say it was meaningful in any way.

Was it enjoyable? Yes, in a sense I can say it was, at times. But can I say I genuinely enjoy watching Netflix for so many hours? I'm not sure.

Was it challenging? No. Though I watch movies in English and Japanese and don't always understand them one hundred percent, I wouldn't exactly call it challenging.

Was it memorable? No. I will have created no valuable memories from watching Netflix. In truth, I could spend hours watching TV or Netflix every day—thousands, if not tens of thousands of hours over my lifetime—and have basically created no positive memories from having done so.

Did it enhance my self-worth? No. If anything, it made me feel bad about myself after a while.

Was it effective? No. I did not actively engage in it as part of my work or study, so this doesn't apply. It's certainly not an effective use of my time.

Was it healthy? No. There is nothing remotely healthy about lying on the couch, watching a screen for hours on end.

To conclude, while watching movies on Netflix once in a while might be fine, based on the seven criteria mentioned above, in this specific situation, I cannot consider it an effective use of my time.

Now, one of the main reasons I wasted so much time on Netflix is because I hadn't filled my schedule with more meaningful activities. So, I figured out that adding extra activities to my evenings would prevent me from wasting so much time.

So, I sat at my desk, took a pen and a sheet of paper, and wrote down all the wonderful things I could be doing instead of wasting so much time watching Netflix. I love studying, so I scheduled time to study Estonian and Japanese each day. I also started an online course on economics and signed up for a course on how to learn more effectively. Meanwhile, I unsubscribed from Netflix and removed distractions by blocking Facebook, YouTube and other websites on my computer. While I will probably relapse in the future, my current program is working pretty well so far.

The lesson here is, whenever you try to remove a toxic activity or behavior, you need to replace it with something else that is both more productive and more enjoyable. Make sure your new activity incorporates some of the criteria mentioned previously. That is, it should be meaningful, enjoyable, memorable, self-worth enhancing, effective and/or health-enhancing. The more exciting and meaningful the activity is, the better. For example, your activity could be part of an exciting long-term goal or dream. Perhaps, you want to:

- Study Spanish because you'd like to move to Spain one day,
- Learn how to play the piano simply for the joy of music,
- Write articles, poems or books, or
- Bake cakes for your family and friends.

Whatever you may be interested in, when you learn to use your time more effectively, you can accomplish almost anything you desire. And the stronger and deeper your desire is, the more motivated you'll be to do the work every day. Once you've built effective systems to ensure you remain consistent, you'll become unstoppable.

Now, let's see what an example of an effective use of your time may look like.

I've been living in Estonia for over a year and a half now, but I barely know any Estonian. I spent months wondering whether I should learn the language. I kept telling myself, "the population is so small, and most Estonians speak English so why should I bother?" Conversely, I wanted to become part of the society, which required me to speak the language. So, instead of wasting hours every day on unproductive activities, I finally decided to learn Estonian. I downloaded an app called *Speakly* and put a daily routine in place. I also hired a private teacher.

Now, compared to watching Netflix, how good a use of my time is studying Estonia? Using the same criteria, let's work it out.

Is it meaningful? I would say yes since it will allow me to use Estonian in my daily life and feel more at home.

Is it challenging? Yes. I have to learn a whole new language and deal with new sounds I'm not used to hearing. Estonian isn't easy!

Is it enjoyable? Yes, I enjoy learning foreign languages and the app I'm using makes it fun and easy.

Is it memorable? Not really. However, speaking Estonian may allow me to create great memories when I make new Estonian friends.

Does it enhance my self-worth? Yes, there's absolutely nothing wrong with learning a new language. Also, being able to speak Estonian will help me to feel better about myself (as opposed to feeling guilty for *not* speaking the language).

Is it effective? Yes. I think the app I'm using in combination with my private lessons should allow me to make progress faster.

Is it health-enhancing? Not really. However, learning something new is really good for my brain.

Overall, we can say that studying Estonian in my specific case is a fairly effective use of my time.

The bottom line is, with the help of the above seven criteria, you can increase the (subjective) value you put in each unit of time you spend subsequently.

What about you? How could you increase the value you get from your time? How could you use it more effectively, every day, so that you can achieve your goals and dreams? What new activities could you start focusing on? What unproductive activities could you eliminate once and for all?

* * *

Action step

- Using your action guide, look at all the activities you engage in during a typical day/week. (To help you, review the time log you created earlier.)

- Then, using the seven criteria described above, assess how much value you're actually gaining from each activity.
- Finally, select one unproductive activity and replace it with a new more meaningful one.

PART IV

MAKING EFFECTIVE USE OF YOUR TIME

1

HOW TO INCREASE YOUR TIME

How would you feel if you could multiply time so that you can achieve much more?

Of course, in reality, we only have twenty-four hours in each day. And I'm not telling you to sleep faster as Arnold Schwarzenegger might suggest. However, they are many things you can do to make better use of your time (or other people's time), so that you can "multiply" your time. In this section, we'll cover a few of them.

A. Borrowing time

While it's true you only have twenty-four hours in each day, nothing prevents you from borrowing time from other people around you. By this, I mean asking for help more consistently and more effectively.

For instance, whenever you tackle a new task or project, rather than figuring out how to do it all by yourself, why not ask others for help? When I don't know how to do something, I always start by asking myself the following questions:

- What exactly am I trying to achieve?
- Do I know anyone with the answers to this question?
- Do I know anyone who knows someone with the answer?

Here's an example of what I mean:

I wanted to translate my books into Spanish, German and French, but I kept procrastinating. I thought it would take me hours to find the right translators. First, I would have to go on a site like Upwork to find experienced translators. Then, I would need to give them each a test before I could select the best candidate. So instead, I asked myself who has already translated their book in these languages. Then, I contacted my friend Richard, who gave the names and contact details of his Spanish, German and French translator. Done!

More recently, I asked my friend Scott if his book cover designer was looking for clients. I've recently started working with this designer. Let's hope the results will meet my expectations.

Now, I'm not telling you to use other people to your advantage and never give anything back in return. In fact, I've helped Richard and Scott quite a bit in the past. I'm just suggesting you develop the habit of asking for help whenever you need it.

Funnily enough, I gave that same advice to one entrepreneur friend. The last time I met her at a dinner, I notice she was getting help from three or four other entrepreneurs. So, I told her, "It's like you have your own board of administration. That's amazing!". She replied, "You were the one who advised me to ask people for help." Fair enough!

The point is, build the habit of identifying the people with the answers to your questions or problems, and approach them first before doing anything else. Let's give a few more examples:

- You want to start investing your money but don't know how. Ask your friend who is already doing very well financially (if you have one).
- You want to create a company but aren't sure how to go about it. Ask your friend who already owns several companies.
- You want to learn a foreign language and make progress fast. Ask your friend who speaks several languages what they recommend you do.

- And so on.

When you build the habit of asking for help, you'll be able to save yourself a great deal of time and hassle, and you will achieve your goals or complete your projects faster than you otherwise would.

* * *

Action step

- Make a list of ten friends, colleagues or acquaintances you're the closest to.
- Next to each name, write down what particular skills they possess.
- Then, imagine that you could upload their brain directly into yours, and ask yourself what knowledge or skills would you like to receive from them?

B. Thinking smartly

Time is one of your most valuable resources. You *must* use it well. And the best way to do this is by learning to think smartly so that you can make better decisions. So, concretely, what does thinking smartly mean?

It means:

- Shortening your learning curve,
- Adopting a mastery mindset,
- Asking yourself empowering questions,
- Approaching your tasks smartly, and
- Scheduling thinking time.

Now, let's look at each of these points in greater detail.

a. Shortening your learning curve

You can choose to spend a lot of time trying to figure something out, or you can choose the easier path: learning from people who've already figured it out. As we mentioned before, it could be by asking for help, but it could also be by watching video tutorials online, buying courses, hiring a coach or working with a mentor.

You do not have time to figure out everything by yourself. If you want to achieve your biggest goals, you must try to accelerate your progress by shortening the learning curve. To do so, you must develop the ability to find the right information. I believe the key to achieving almost anything can be boiled down to the following two things:

1. Your ability to find the right information, and

2. Your ability to apply it consistently until you achieve results.

Fortunately, thanks to the internet, we're only ever a few clicks away from all the knowledge in the world. But, paradoxically, because information has become a commodity, we fail to value it. We consume book after book and course after course but extract little value from them. We know many things but only intellectually. In other words, we have knowledge but no wisdom.

Therefore, make sure you value the information you have access to, which is priceless. Then, use it to skyrocket your productivity and achieve your goals faster. Remember, knowledge without action is valueless.

Now, let's see how you can apply what you learn effectively by adopting a mastery mindset.

If you want to learn, in detail, how to apply the information you gather to achieve tangible results, you can also read my book *Master Your Focus*.

b. Adopting a mastery mindset

Many people keep jumping from one apparently exciting thing to the next. They read book after book, join seminar after seminar, and buy course after course—but they never seem to get anywhere. Such behavior is often referred to as *Shiny Object Syndrome*.

Because time is one of the scarcest resources on earth, you cannot allow yourself to behave in such a way. When you jump from one new fad to the next without anything to show for your work, in effect, you're squandering your time. What you must do instead is to learn to focus until you achieve tangible results. To do so, you must adopt a "mastery mindset".

What is a "mastery mindset" you ask? Let's find out!

First, I must mention that the mastery mindset is not a new concept, and I certainly didn't invent it. People such as the famous coach, Tony Robbins, have been teaching this model for years. However, too few people truly understand how fundamental the concept really is.

Once you truly understand how it works and begin to adopt it, everything will change for you. Instead of running around like a hamster on a wheel, you'll start obtaining results like never before, and you'll start hitting your goals.

The 7 pillars of the mastery mindset

I believe there are seven pillars you need to adopt in order to develop a mastery mindset. Let's review each of them, shall we?

1) Mastering repetition

Every successful person is a master of repetition. For example, the hugely successful Olympic swimmer, Michael Phelps, didn't miss a single day of training between the ages of twelve and eighteen. In fact, he swam more than 2,100 days in a row. Martial arts experts practice the same move thousands of times. And kids learn how to write by copying the alphabet over and over. In fact, it is impossible to become proficient at anything without first embracing the philosophy of repetition.

Repetition is the process that allows you to assimilate anything and, over time, become highly skilled in the process. If you're a driver, do you remember the first time you sat behind the steering wheel? You probably felt overwhelmed by the large amount of new information you had to process. You might even have wondered whether you would ever be able to drive. But, after spending many hours practicing, the skill became automatic. This demonstrates that you have effectively transferred the driving process from your conscious to your subconscious mind. This is what repetition and mastery are about: repeating something so many times it becomes second nature.

The point is, knowing things only intellectually is not enough. To become truly adept at a skill, you must practice over and over until the skill becomes second nature. You must adopt the mindset that you will practice as many times as necessary until you achieve the results you want.

2) Mastering the fundamentals

Most people believe they know more than they actually do. Then, when nothing seems to work, they're left confused. This is because their fundamental skills are weak. They may have been avoiding learning a specific skill because they think it's not important or because they were too eager to move on to the next topic. But the devil is often in the details. By overlooking one small detail after another, many people end up miles away from their intended destination.

Do you really know everything you need to know about your goals? Have you applied everything you've learned? And have you done so consistently?

Once you have a specific goal in mind, you must learn everything you need to know about it. For instance, you must learn:

- How to perform weight exercises properly or you will not get the results you want and may even hurt yourself in the process,
- How to study effectively or you'll forget most of what you learn, or
- About healthy food, or you'll think you're eating healthily when you aren't.

The most successful people on earth are obsessed with learning the fundamentals and there is a reason for this. Without strong fundamentals, your potential for growth is limited. Without the fundamentals, you can't become great, let alone world-class at whatever you do.

Despite the fact he was already the best golfer in the world, Tiger Woods wanted to improve his game. To this end, he hired a coach, who told him he would have to change his swing. Yes, Tiger Woods decided he needed to relearn the fundamentals. Interestingly, Tiger Woods' situation is not uncommon. When seeking to improve their performance, many world-class athletes return to the basics. This enables them to rebuild their craft from the ground up and take it to the next level.

To master the fundamentals, you need to:

- Follow a step-by-step approach,
- Apply everything you learn, and
- Return to the fundamentals as often as necessary.

Let's review these three components.

Following a step-by-step approach

Without clear guidance and accountability, you'll find it difficult to learn anything on your own. You need a blueprint, showing you what to do, step-by-step. The more structured your learning, the easier it will be to make progress.

This is something I've personally been struggling with. Eager to make progress, I often try to learn as quickly as possible, without giving myself enough time to assimilate the information or enough practice to build strong foundations. If you identify yourself as a seminar junkie, don't worry, you can change—read on.

Whenever you enroll in a step-by-step course, I invite you to do the following:

- Decide exactly how long you'll spend on the course by setting a specific schedule.
- Set aside blocks of time every day or every week. For

instance, you could decide to dedicate one hour to the course every weekday.

- Make sure you complete all the exercises in each lesson before moving on to the next.
- Avoid taking more than one or two courses at a time. It's unlikely you'll be able to achieve great results with too many courses on your plate.

So, stick to one or two courses, schedule them and commit to obtaining tangible results before moving onto the next module or the next course.

Applying everything you learn

To master the fundamentals and make progress, you implement what you learn. Without implementation, no significant results are possible. Therefore, whatever source of information you use, make sure you work on every actionable item available. This entails:

- Doing everything your coach suggests,
- Completing all the exercises in the course you take, and
- Working through all the exercises outlined in the books you read (this one, for example).

Now, I understand you can't always take action on all the information you consume. What you can do, however, is ensure that, for any major goal you set, take consistent action on everything you learn.

Returning to the fundamentals when necessary

Have you ever failed to achieve tangible results with a course or a book you bought? If so, you might need to revisit the fundamentals. Sometimes, overlooking one small detail can make all the difference between success and failure. It is also important that you learn to question yourself rather than the validity of the information you consume.

Once you've done your best to select high-quality information, avoid questioning its validity. Trust the program and take consistent action on it.

Ask yourself the following questions:

- Have I really completed all the exercises diligently?
- Have I missed anything?

You'll often find you've neglected something. Remember, to become a master, you must practice everything until you become living proof of it.

For instance, let's assume you bought a training course that offers a step-by-step method to sell your services but, after multiple attempts, you have yet to close a sale. Now, what may be missing? Are you following the script to the letter or are you trying to be fancy? Did you discard a few things you thought weren't important? Avoid doing this. Instead, stick to the method exactly until you make your first sale. Remember, if others have used the method successfully, so can you.

3) Having faith in the process

Do you have faith in the process you are following? If you hire a coach, take a course or buy a book and believe it's *not* going to work, you've already lost half of the battle. You must have faith in the process and commit to doing whatever it takes to make it work for you. Remember, if others can succeed, so can you. Thus, make it a must to achieve positive results and never give up until you do. You want to build a successful track record with any product you use. For instance:

- If you bought a course to help you find coaching clients, do whatever it takes to win the first client. Then remember that if you can find one client, you can find many more.
- If you bought a program on how to publish an eBook on Amazon, stick to the process and make sure you publish at least one book.

- If you enrolled in a diet program, stick to it until you lose at least your first few pounds.

Avoid mixing information

Avoid combining information from various courses. Once you find the best source of information, stick to that particular process. If you want, you can change your approach and try other courses later on but, for now, it's important you develop the habit of sticking to something until you gain success.

4) Being willing to learn

Your ability to humble yourself and to remain coachable is one of the keys to effective learning. The more personal responsibility you take for the results you achieve, the faster you will grow. Always be willing to learn and take personal responsibility before blaming others for any lack of progress.

The legendary investor, Warren Buffet, has been reading five or six hours per day for decades. Although in his nineties, he still spends hours each day trying to master his craft. This is because he understands there is always more to learn. Even the best of the best in their field learn continuously, and so should you.

The bottom line is that you must keep learning and growing until you achieve the results you want. If you let your ego and pride stand in the way, you'll slow your progress.

If you've been struggling to obtain certain results for years, you can blame others as much as you want, but the only constant in the equation is you. Although you are most likely the problem, as it happens, you are also the solution. So be open to learning and you might find everything starts changing for you.

If something isn't working for you, I recommend you ask yourself:

- Might I have been wrong here?
- What could I do differently?
- What is the real bottleneck holding back my success?

- Who can I turn to for advice?

5) Embracing long-term thinking

As we discussed earlier, the ability to think long term is one of the best predictors of success. When you focus on your long-term vision and act accordingly every day, you are far more likely to create the life you want. Therefore, if your current daily actions aren't moving you closer to your vision, start questioning your methods.

Masters always have a long-term plan. They know they cannot excel at anything without first spending years working on their craft. What about you? Are you a master? If you're unsure, look at the tasks you've completed recently. Are these tasks contributing to your long-term vision or are they distractions? Are you creating your future proactively, or are you reacting to your environment?

Learn to think in the long term and, over time, you will notice a significant improvement in your performance.

6) Being consistent

Another key characteristic of a master is their consistency. Consistency is focus repeated every day in the pursuit of a long-term vision. Without consistency, your focus will be short-lived and have little-to-no power. Without a solid focus, you can't master anything.

In other words, consistency is using your ax to hit your big tree—your goal—at the exact same spot over and over until the tree topples. Consistency is practicing the same kick ten thousand times until it becomes deadly.

To give you real life examples, it is:

- Creating and uploading YouTube videos every day for years,
- Writing every day and publishing a book every two months for years,
- Waking up at the same time every single day, or
- Calling prospects every single morning.

Consistency allows you to build momentum over time. It boosts your ability to focus, increases your self-esteem and skyrockets your productivity. To become a master, simply start by doing something consistently every day, no matter how small the action may be.

Also, understand there is no such thing as one hundred percent consistency. Nobody is perfect. Therefore, avoid beating yourself up whenever you fall off track. Instead, show self-compassion and refocus on your goal.

7) Focusing

Instead of scattering their focus, masters invest it wisely to design the life they want. Remember, you can only focus on one thing at a time. When you fail to concentrate your attention on something that improves your life, you move away from the life you want to create. Eventually, what you focus on consistently day after day creates your life. So, make certain you get it right. Otherwise, ten years from now, you will end up in a totally different place from the one you intended.

Commit to a few actions and, relying on the mastery mindset, stick to those actions until you achieve the desired outcome.

You won't become a master overnight but, by developing a mastery mindset, over the coming months and years you will find yourself achieving better results faster than ever before.

You can be either a master or a dabbler. The choice is yours.

c. Asking yourself empowering questions

Our brain is like a search engine. Whatever questions we ask, it will try to produce the best answers possible. Unfortunately, most of us ask silly questions and, as result, receive silly answers.

What about you? What questions do you ask yourself? Are they serving you? Or are they preventing you from achieving your goals?

Ultimately, the quality of the questions you ask yourself determines the quality of your life. So, make sure you ask yourself smart ones. Below are examples of quality questions you can ask yourself.

Questions regarding the way you use your time

- What does "using time effectively" mean to me?
- What do I need to do today/this week to live a life without regrets?
- What does my ideal day look like?

More specific questions regarding productivity

- What exactly am I trying to accomplish here? What does the end result look like for this task or project?
- What's the number one bottleneck in my life right now? What specific things could I do to eliminate it?
- What's the best way to approach this task? How do I know it's the best way?
- Who has the answer to this problem? Who can help me achieve this goal?

More generally speaking, the following types of questions are invaluable.

"What if" questions

These questions tap into one of your most precious assets—your imagination. As human beings, we are the only species on earth with the ability to project ourselves into the future and come back with valuable insights, empowering states of mind or specific plans of actions. Thus, the first step to achieving anything is to use the power of your imagination. And it starts by asking yourself, "What if".

- What if I can achieve my biggest goal in the next five to ten years?
- What if I can design a career I absolutely love?
- What if I can attract a wonderful partner into my life?
- What if X, Y or Z is possible for me?

"How" questions

These questions foster creativity and will open yourself up to new possibilities and ways to solve your issues.

- How can I achieve this goal in the next ninety days?
- How can I work fewer hours while getting more done?
- How can I approach this project the most effective way possible?
- How can I retire ten years early?
- How can I make more money?

Similar questions are:

- What can I do...?
- What would I need to do...?
- What would it take to...?

"Who" questions

While being resourceful and self-reliant is important, there is nothing wrong with asking for help whenever it's needed. Start by asking yourself the following questions:

- Who has the answer to this question?
- Who has solved this problem before?
- Who has already achieved this goal?
- Who do I really want to spend more time with?
- Who has the same values as me?

There are over seven billion people on this planet and with the internet you're only one click away from many of them. Many people have the skills, experience, resources, money, or connections you need to achieve any of your goals or dreams. Learn to tap into that collective intelligence.

To conclude, what you keep thinking about every day will tend to become your reality in the long term. And what determines for a large part where your focus goes, are the questions you're asking yourself. So, make sure you ask yourself empowering questions on a daily basis.

d. Approaching your tasks smartly

Productivity isn't about completing as many tasks as possible. This might work for simple jobs but for most of us, we're actually expected to do some thinking. To use the words of the management consultant, Peter Drucker, you must do the right things, not things right. In other words, you must ensure that what you're working on is the most important thing you could be doing right now.

The 7-Step process below will help to ensure you approach any task as effectively as possible. Follow this process until it becomes second nature.

Step 1. Prioritizing your task

Before you even start doing anything, ask yourself the following questions:

- If I could do only one thing today, which task would have the most impact?
- Is this task moving me closer to my main goal?
- Do I really need to do this right now, or should I do it later?

You want to train yourself to think in terms of priorities and keep an eye on the bigger picture. Losing perspective and forgetting your overall strategy is the fastest way to waste time on unimportant tasks.

Step 2. Assessing the validity of your task

To ensure the task is something you actually need to undertake, ask yourself the following questions:

- Do I really need to do this task?
- Is right now the best time? What would happen if I delay it for a week? A month? Forever?
- Am I working on it because I need to or because it makes me

feel good? In short, am I working on this task as a way to escape from what I really should be doing?

There is nothing more unproductive than doing something you didn't need to do in the first place. Answering the above questions can help you to avoid making such a mistake.

Step 3. Clarifying what needs to be done

Before starting on a task, be certain you know exactly what is required. To do so, ask yourself:

- What exactly do I need to do here?
- What am I trying to accomplish?
- What does the finished product look like?

You need to be specific. By knowing exactly what the output needs to be, you'll be able to optimize your approach and tackle the task more effectively.

Step 4. Determining whether you should be the person doing it

You have strengths, but you also have weaknesses. Whenever possible, try to delegate any task someone else can do better, faster or more cheaply than you.

Ask yourself the following questions:

- Is this task worth my time?
- Can someone else do it better than me? If so, can I ask for help?
- What would happen if I simply remove/postpone this task?
- Do I enjoy working on this task? Does it motivate me?

Little by little, you want to get into the habit of outsourcing everything you're not good at and focusing only on the high-value tasks at which you excel. Your time is more valuable than money. So, learn to use money to save time.

Step 5. Finding out the most effective way to tackle a task

As Abraham Lincoln said, *"Give me six hours to chop a tree and I will spend the first four sharpening the ax."*

Just taking a few minutes to consider the best way to approach the task can save you so much time in the long run. Ask yourself the following questions:

- What tool(s) can I use, people can I ask or method can I rely on to complete this task as efficiently and effectively as possible?
- What skill(s) could I learn to help me complete this task faster in the future?

For instance, let's say you've been asked to create a presentation at work. Rather than creating it from scratch, why not reuse or modify materials from a previous presentation? Always aim to utilize existing templates, methods or knowledge. Be smart. The last thing you want to do is reinvent the wheel.

To sum up, before tackling any task, take a few minutes to work out the best possible way to approach it. This habit alone will save you a great deal of time and effort down the road.

Step 6. Batching the task with other similar tasks

Some tasks can be combined with other tasks that require the same type of effort or preparation. For instance, many YouTubers block one full day a week or even an entire month to record YouTube videos, as opposed to creating one video every day. This reduces setup time and makes the process more efficient.

Ask yourself:

- Can I batch this task with other similar tasks to boost my productivity?

Step 7. Automating/systemizing your task

Finally, you should look for ways to automate or systemize your task, especially if it's a repetitive one.

Ask yourself:

- Can I create templates to reuse every time I work on this task or similar ones? (For instance, you could design templates for the specific emails, presentations or documents you need to create over and over.)
- Can I create a checklist? (Checklists provide you with specific steps to follow, making it less likely you will become distracted.)

e. Scheduling thinking time

To make effective use of your time it is also essential you give yourself time to think, even if it's just thirty minutes each week. Over the long term, this will save you a lot of time. I encourage you to ask yourself the following questions:

- Am I satisfied with the way I used my time this week?
- What is working and not working for me right now? Why?
- If I keep doing what I'm doing this week, will I achieve my most important goals? If not, what needs to change? Starting next week, what is the one thing I could do differently to move me toward my goals most effectively?
- What valuable lesson(s) did I learn about myself this week?
- What's my biggest bottleneck, right now? What obstacle(s) can I remove right now to improve my results most significantly?

Action step

Complete the exercises below using your action guide:

- Select one goal you'd most like to achieve. Now, write down what you could do to shorten the learning curve and reach it as quickly as possible.

- Write down what you would do differently if you were to adopt a mastery mindset.
- Come up with at least one question in each category and answer it ("What if", "How", and "Who").
- Choose one task and go through the 7-Step process to approach it smartly (whether in real life or in your mind). Follow these seven steps whenever you work on a task.
- Block off thirty to sixty minutes this week to think. To help you think, try answering the questions mentioned in this book.

C. Improving your skills

Time is limited, but we can all improve the amount of work we accomplish in the time we have. An effective way to "multiply" time is by improving our current skills or developing new ones. I truly believe that one of the most important skills we can develop is the ability to learn better and faster. This is especially true in our ever-changing world. And this rate of change is unlikely to slow any time soon. If anything, the speed of change will only keep increasing.

When it comes to improving your current set of skills, the first thing you should do is identify the skills you need to work on first. If you improved one of your existing skills, which one would boost your productivity the most? After improving this particular skill, you should identify the new skills you could acquire to become even more productive at work.

For instance, many of us spend an incredible amount of time in front of the computer researching information, typing reports, replying to emails and so on.

- If you're using a spreadsheet at work, perhaps you could take a course to improve your skills.
- If you're a slow typist, you could work on increasing your typing speed.
- If you're spending too much time answering emails, you could set aside a specific (and limited) time to answer them.
- If you waste a lot of time search for files on your computer, you could improve your organization skills.

The point is, to get more out of your time, you need to start improving your skills. The more skilled you become, the better you will perform. So, keep learning.

* * *

Action step

Using your action guide, write down the key skills you could learn or improve on in order to boost your productivity long term.

Practicing new skills the correct way

When you are trying to improve your skills, you must do so deliberately, using what is often referred to as "deliberate practice". That is, you must practice with intense focus and with a specific intent in mind. You must know why you're doing something and the outcome you hope to achieve from it.

People often say they have X years of experience in a certain field, but that's misleading. What they're really saying is that they've been working in a specific field for X years. However, the truth is probably this:

They improved their skills for two or three years and then kept doing the things they already knew, over and over again for years, and with only marginal improvements here and there.

In this regard, the following study is eye-opening:

According to researchers at Harvard Medical School, doctors with decades of experience don't seem to provide better patient care than those with just a few years of experience.

You would expect a doctor with decades of experience to be significantly more skilled than a young one, right? However, according to the Harvard study, this doesn't appear to be the case. The same applies to nurses, and I suspect, in many other professions.

My point is, to become great at anything, you must continuously improve your skills—and you must do so deliberately. But this is hard work, which is why most people choose not to do so.

Now, what exactly is "deliberate practice"?

In their book *Peak, Secrets from The New Science of Expertise*, Anders Ericsson and Robert Pool explain that deliberate practice:

1. Builds skills for which effective training techniques have already been established,
2. Takes place outside of your comfort zone, requires significant effort and is generally not enjoyable,
3. Involves specific, well-defined goals,
4. Requires your full attention and conscious actions,
5. Entails regular feedback,
6. Both creates and relies on effective mental representation, and
7. Almost always involves working on existing skills or building new ones by focusing specifically on some aspect of those skills that need to be improved.

Let's give a concrete example. Benjamin Franklin wanted to improve his writing skills. He focused on improving three specific skills—his writing style, his vocabulary and his sense of organization.

In a nutshell, here is Benjamin Franklin's schedule for deliberate practice:

- **Writing style:** He made notes on articles from Spectator—a high-quality newspaper—which he would use to rewrite the articles a few days later. He would then compare his version with the original article and modify it accordingly.
- **Vocabulary:** He rewrote Spectator essays in verse and then in prose, to compare his vocabulary with the original article.
- **Organization:** He wrote summaries of every sentence in a particular article on separate sheets of paper. He would then wait a few weeks before challenging himself to write the article in the correct order and then he compared his work to the original.

He was very intentional in the way he learned, using "deliberate practice", as we can confirm below.

- Benjamin Franklin's tedious studies required a great deal of effort and were probably not much fun (#2).

- It involved defined goals such as rewriting specific articles until he could reproduce the original (#3).
- It required both his full attention and conscious actions (#4).
- He also received immediate feedback by looking at the original article to determine how well he performed (#5).
- Through consistent practice, he created a mental representation of patterns of information held in long-term memory. In short, we can say he transferred new skills to his subconscious so that he could use them automatically whenever sitting down to write (#6).
- Finally, he was working on improving a specific skill (his writing ability) by focusing on specific aspects of it (improving his writing style, increasing the richness of his vocabulary and enhancing his organization skills) (#7).

Whether or not he actually used existing methods to improve his skills is hard to say. For the most part, we can assume he invented techniques to meet his specific needs. This shows how dedicated and determined he was to become a better writer.

When you adopt deliberate practice, you'll increase the value of each unit of time you dedicate to that purpose. In short, you'll make better use of your time and will progress more quickly. Such practice will inevitably boost your ability to focus.

Below are some of the things that can help you design a deliberate practice:

- Identify a specific program, course or manual used by people who achieved the goal you're after.
- Hire a coach.
- Find a mentor.
- Ask a friend who has achieved similar results for advice.

* * *

Action step

How could you use deliberate practice to improve your current skills or acquire new ones? Answer this question using your action guide.

To conclude, you can increase the value of each unit of time by improving your thinking abilities. By looking at the bigger picture and being more strategic, every action you take will become more impactful. Instead of being busy, you'll become highly effective.

Now, let's see what you can do to "store" your time.

2

HOW TO STORE TIME

As we now know, time is one of our most precious assets. Every second that passes is gone forever. And, unfortunately, we cannot store our time for later use.

Or can we?

Although we cannot stop time, there is a specific way we can "buy back" time to have more of it available in the future. The tool that enables us to do this is money.

A. Using money to store time

While some people strive to make more money so that they can increase their social status, gain power or buy luxury items, in my opinion, this is not where money's true power lies.

The power of money lies in its ability to store our energy and time so that we can use it in the future. In fact, accumulating money allows us to buy back time. To regain control over your time, you must understand what money is and how you can use it to buy your way to freedom.

For example, if you can save money each month, you might be able to retire a few years (or even a few decades) earlier than most people.

This is what the proponents of the F.I.R.E. movement work toward (F.I.R.E. stands for Financial Independence, Retire Early). The money you saved can be invested so that it works for you and increases over time.

I invite you to see money as freedom; the freedom to make better use of your scarcest resource, your time. Think about it this way: money enables you to store the fruits of your labor. Without it, you would be forever doomed to work to meet your basic needs. Each dollar you save gives you an opportunity to reclaim part of your future. In short, saving money gives you options. When you're able to save enough of it, you can decide to take a break from work, invest the money in a side business or change your career for a more enjoyable job that may not pay as well.

In a way, because it multiplies your options and enables you to buy back your time, saving money might be the ultimate productivity tool.

On the other hand, you can earn a lot of money, but unless you're able to save and invest some of it each month, you'll end up running like a hamster in a wheel, never being in control of your time. You'll always be one crisis away from losing everything (your job, your home your lifestyle, et cetera).

It's even worse when you're in debt. Being in debt forces you to utilize your time to repay your creditors. This time cannot be used to meet your needs, nor can it be stored for future use.

Here's the point. Money isn't evil. Money allows you to store the fruit of your labor and use it to buy back time. To become a master of your time, you should reassess your relationship with money. Understand that money is stored time. Then, begin to save and invest more money so that you can reclaim your time at a later date.

Action step

Write down what you would do if you could store time (for example, retiring early, changing your career, dedicating more time to your hobbies, et cetera).

B. Becoming a smart consumer

We often buy things without checking whether they're worth our money (and time). To assess whether you should buy something, calculate how many hours you need to work in order to buy it. Let's say you want to purchase a new phone that costs $900. If you earn $15 per hour, you'll need to work 60 hours before you can acquire it. Now, is that a lot or a little? I don't know. It depends on how useful you think the phone will be. Perhaps, buying a less expensive model would be good enough for you. Or, perhaps, you absolutely love that particular phone and *want* to buy it, irrespective of the cost.

Understanding hidden opportunity costs

It is important to understand that with every purchase you make there is an opportunity cost. You cannot both spend your money on a new phone and save it. Each dollar spent is a dollar not invested. In other words, each dollar spent is accumulated time you're voluntarily giving away (i.e., the time you've "stored" by making that money through work).

And because the money you invest can increase multifold over several decades, what you choose to buy or not to buy is much more important than you think.

For instance, let's say you've just got your first job out of college. Excited to be making money and eager to reward yourself, you decided to buy yourself a nice car. To do so, you take a $30,000 loan that you will repay over the course of several years. There's nothing wrong with that, is there? After all, you're making money now. However, this seemingly inoffensive purchase comes with huge opportunity costs.

Let's say the total cost of the loan, including interest, is $40,000. Then, let's assume it will take you eight years to pay the loan back in its entirety. In this case, you'll have to pay back $417 per month, which is $417 you won't be able to use for anything else each month.

Now, what if you chose to invest the $417 each month for eight years at an annual return of five percent after inflation? By the end of the eight years, you'll have amassed $47,783. But that's not the most impressive thing. Imagine you decide to let that money compound over a few decades, never touching it before retirement. Let's be conservative and use thirty years. At the end of this thirty-year period, you'll have amassed $206,515.98. Not bad, eh?

Having this much extra in the bank will give you more options. For example, you might be able to:

- Retire a little earlier than planned, or
- Have a higher monthly pension when you retire.

My point is this. Saved money happens to be stored time. By saving or investing your money instead of spending it, you can buy back time in whichever way you please. For instance, you can:

- Outsource unpleasant tasks to free more time to do things you enjoy,
- Retire early and dedicate that extra time to your hobbies, or
- Change career and go for a more meaningful job, and so on.

You can always make more money, but you can never acquire more time. Therefore, make sure you use your money as a tool to store time. And if you want to both spend more *and* save more, you must find a way to increase your income.

In the table below, I have added a few more scenarios to give you an idea of how powerful the compound effect is. You'll see what happens if you earn a seven—instead of a five—percent return, or invest your income for forty instead of thirty years.

	$47,783 ($417 x 8 years)	
	5% annual return	**7% annual return**
After 30 years	$206,515.98	$363,737.45
After 40 years	$336,392.77	$715,526.62

I've also included another example showing you how much you would need to invest over a forty-year period to accumulate $1 million (assuming a seven percent annual return). Spoiler: you need to invest $390 per month.

$390/month investment with a 7% annual return	
After 10 years	US$69,261.16
After 20 years	US$205,508.35
After 30 years	US$473,527.20
After 40 years	**US$1,000,760.83**
After 50 years	US$2,037,909.20

Note that the average historical return of the S&P 500 since its creation in 1926 is slightly below ten percent, before inflation. (The S&P 500 is a stock market index that measures the value of the 500 largest companies traded on U.S. stock markets.)

Action step

- Write down a few things you'd like to buy.
- Then, calculate how many hours you must work to buy them.
- Finally, see if there are any alternative options. Can you buy something less expensive while getting more or less the same benefits? Or should you merely give up on buying those things because you can use the money more effectively?

3

DISCONNECTING TIME FROM MONEY

As our old friend Warren Buffet once said, *"If you don't find a way to make money while you sleep, you will work until you die."*

Time is much scarcer than money. Now, I understand that if you have money issues right now, it might definitely not seem that way, but the more you learn to value your time, the more money you'll likely make over a long enough period. It won't happen tomorrow, but if you're patient enough it eventually will.

In this section, I'd like to discuss the importance of disconnecting your time from the money you make. There is a large amount of work involved in mastering this concept, but I will give you a brief overview to help you shift your mindset regarding time and money.

To learn more on the topic you can start by reading, *Rich Dad, Poor Dad* by Robert T. Kiyosaki or *The Millionaire Fastlane* by MJ DeMarco.

A. Saving money vs. saving time

Which of these statements do you relate to the most:

- I use time to save money, or
- I use money to save time.

As you learn to master your time, you'll come to realize that the key isn't to use your time (scarce) to save money (abundant), but to use your money (abundant) to save your time (scarce). This is because time is the scarcer resource of the two. Again, if you're not making much money right now, you'll find it difficult to do so, but please bear with me.

The first step to value your time more is to calculate how much an hour of your time is actually worth. To do so, you can simply divide your salary by the number of hours you work each month. For instance, if you take home $4,000 per month and work forty hours a week, your hourly wage is around $25.

Now you know how much an hour of your time is worth approximately, you can start assessing whether you're making the most of your time right now.

For example, some people spend hours collecting coupons to save a few dollars on their groceries. Others line up for hours in front of a store to "take advantage" of a special promotion. These people do not understand the true value of their time. As a result, they don't make good use of it. Unless they change their mindset, they probably won't make a lot of money either.

On the other hand, people who value their time will not spend hours simply to save a few bucks. Instead, they might use that time to work on their side hustle, learn new skills or simply engage in their favorite hobbies. (If your hobby is standing in queues or collecting coupons, perhaps you're doing the right thing after all).

The more you value your time, the more you'll likely end up making money over the long term.

What about you? Are you giving more importance to money than to time? If so, what could you do specifically to change that?

The point is, practice using money to save time, not the other way around.

Action step

- Write down all the ways you're giving more importance to money than to time.
- Now, write down what you would do differently if you perceived time as far scarcer than money.

B. Exchanging time for money

Most people sell their time for money. That is, they're getting paid per hour worked. Now, there is nothing wrong with that and it's certainly convenient for many people. But the problem is, we only have twenty-four hours a day and can only work so many hours before needing to rest. Therefore, the amount of money we can make by exchanging our time for money is capped.

But what if you want to work less and/or make more money?

Then, you must stop exchanging your time for money. Or you must make your money work for you instead of the other way around.

To do so, you must use leverage.

C. Leveraging your time

You have two choices: you can either sell your time, or you can leverage it (or use a mix of both).

To put it simply, you sell your time when you're an employee. However, you leverage your time when you:

- Create assets that pay you multiple times (books, online courses, YouTube videos, franchises, et cetera),
- Get paid on a project basis (i.e., deliver a result regardless of how many hours of work it takes you), or
- Use other people's time (hiring employees or freelancers to work for you).

When you do any of the above things, you can potentially increase the value of your time. If a book sells well, you can make more per hour than at a typical salaried job. If your YouTube channel takes off, you can make "passive" income for years. If you get paid by results and can deliver a lot of value with little work, you'll also increase your income. And by hiring people, you can free time to work on high-value tasks that will generate more income. Of course, there is also a risk that things don't work out as planned, but that's all part of the game of risk and reward.

If you truly want to master your time, you must learn to leverage it instead of selling it. Outlined below are the main things you can use to make more effective use of your time:

- Other people's time.
- Other people's money.
- Other people's knowledge.
- Other people's influence, or
- Technology.

a. Other's people time

Your time is scarce but by leveraging other people's time, you can accomplish much more than you would when working alone—and in far less time. As we've already mentioned, you can hire freelancers or employees to help complete your tasks. Doing so can save time which you can then use to work on high-impact tasks you're good at. For instance, I leverage other people's time when I hire:

- Translators,
- Cover designers,
- Editors,
- Narrators, and
- Proofreaders.

In fact, in most cases, I don't have any other choices as I don't possess the skills needed to do these tasks myself. Sure, I could use translation software, design covers myself, ask a friend to edit and proofread my books, and narrate them myself, but I wouldn't get the same level of quality and it wouldn't be sustainable.

You can also use other people's time for other things. For instance, you could hire a house cleaner, a babysitter or a gardener. Then, you could use that extra time to do meaningful things in your personal or professional life.

Here is another example:

A few months ago, I sent a fraction of my cryptocurrencies to a trusted friend who invested them alongside his own. It didn't require more work for him to manage the pool of money and it didn't require any of my time. In short, I leveraged his time while he leveraged my money. Be careful though. I wouldn't advise you to let anyone manage your money unless you trust them completely. And, even so, I would be wary. My friend only managed one percent or so of my total assets.

What about you? If you could leverage other people's time to free extra time for yourself, who would you hire? And what would you do with that extra time?

b. Other people's money

You might not have money, but many people do. Using other people's money might be an effective way to save time. For instance, you could:

- Get a loan from the bank to buy a house or apartment either for your own use or to rent. By doing so, effectively, you're using someone else's money to buy assets that will probably appreciate and/or generate cash flow.
- Raise funds for your company, products or services. My friend Richard, who I mentioned earlier in this book, was able to raise thousands of dollars for one of his books using Kickstarter. This was money he didn't have to earn (i.e., time he was able to save).

The bottom line is, if you can get a loan with a low interest rate wherever you live, perhaps consider taking a mortgage or buying a rental property (make sure you do extensive research beforehand, though). If you need money for an upcoming project, perhaps you can raise funds over the internet.

What about you? Is there any way you could use other people's money in an effective manner?

c. Other people's knowledge

Today, thanks to the internet, we can learn almost anything we desire and often for free. For instance, do you realize that you can read books written by world experts on any topic you desire? These experts put decades of experience inside a few hundred pages just so that you can learn from them.

As I noted earlier, you don't have time to reinvent the wheel. Using other people's knowledge and leveraging their decades of experience will save you precious time:

- Read books from world experts and learn as much as you can from them.
- Leverage the skills and experience of people around you by asking for their help or advice whenever needed.
- Absorb high-quality content and make sure you take action on what you're learning. You want practical wisdom, not intellectual knowledge.

So, how you could use other people's knowledge to save time?

d. Other people's influence

The bigger your network is, the more likely you are to know someone who can help you solve your problems and achieve your goals. For instance, your network can help you find a better job, sell more of your products or services, or create partnerships (among other things).

Thus, don't be afraid to ask for help whenever you need it. Your friends or acquaintances can help you solve problems faster and more effectively than you can by yourself. This will save you a lot of trouble—and a great deal of time.

How could you use your network so as to make better use of your time?

* * *

Action step

Using your action guide, write down one important goal. Then, write down how your network could help you achieve this goal faster.

e. Technology

When it comes to increasing the value of your time, technology can be extremely powerful. It can provide you with incredible leverage. The more you use technology to your advantage, the better. By technology, I mainly mean the internet and everything you can do with it. For instance, you can:

- Sell digital or physical products on Amazon (and many other digital sites),
- Become a seller on eBay,
- Use YouTube to promote your business (or become a full-time Youtuber),
- Leverage Shopify or other services to sell products on your website,
- Use print-on-demand services to sell products,
- Run ads on major platforms to boost your sales (Facebook, YouTube, Amazon, et cetera), or
- Rent your house using Airbnb.

In addition, you can use technology to automate many of your tasks. For instance, you can:

- Use software such as Zapier to automate entire processes (you can connect it to over 1,000 business tools),
- Create advanced Excel spreadsheets to reduce your workload (In his book *Deep Work*, Cal Newport relates how a newly hired financial consultant, Jason Benn, reduced a

report-writing process from six hours to less than one hour by building a new Excel spreadsheet.),

- Use auto-responder services to send emails to new subscribers/clients, or
- Schedule an entire month's worth of social media posts with software such as Buffer.

Personally, I always strive to use technology to simplify my business. To free up my time and help me enjoy more freedom, I want technology to work for me 24/7.

Previously, we've seen that money is a means to store your work so that you can use the fruit of your labor (more time) at a later date. In a sense, the internet is also a means to store your work across time. However, with the internet, you can share it worldwide, 24/7, forever. This is why it's so immensely powerful.

To sum up, because time is so scarce, you should aim to leverage other resources around you to help you make effective use of it. Outsource tasks, ask your friends for help or advice, raise funds, consume educational content and use all the technology available as often as possible.

Now, let's see how you can develop laser-sharp focus and boost your productivity.

PART V

DEVELOPING EXTRAORDINARY FOCUS

You cannot manage time, but you can direct your focus toward the activities that matter the most while time passes. It reminds me of the following quote by the motivational speaker, Earl Nightingale:

"Never give up on a dream just because of the time it will take to accomplish it. The time will pass anyway."

Yes, the time will pass anyway, so you might as well do something with the time you have right now.

What you focus on, and the level of intensity with which you do so, are the most important elements when it comes to increasing your productivity. Making effective use of your time is not about completing one task after the other on a never-ending to-do list. It's not about multitasking either. It's about focusing properly. Focusing enhances the intensity you put into your work, and thus increases the value of each unit of time you use in that way.

Remember, the energy you have each day is severely limited. It acts as a bottleneck on how much you can do. Focus is what enables you to make effective use of that scarce energy instead of allowing it to dissipate. Sadly, most people are not energy efficient, and they lose an incredible amount of energy each day by failing to protect their focus. For instance:

- **They keep switching from one task to another**, preventing their brain from entering a deep state of concentration and wasting a lot of energy in the process.
- **They allow themselves to be interrupted multiple times during the day**, which pulls them out of focus again and again. They then need to expend an enormous amount of energy to refocus on their task.
- **They keep checking their emails**, scrolling their newsfeed on Facebook or checking their phone. This erodes their ability to focus and destroys any momentum they may have been building.
- **They work on unimportant tasks first** and only tackle the most productive tasks later in the day, and only if they have enough willpower, energy and focus to do so (which they often don't).

Gloria Mark, a researcher at the University of California, discovered that, on average, office workers are interrupted every eleven minutes. But where it gets even worse is that they will need around twenty minutes to return to their previous level of concentration.

Multitasking is also a major issue. Clifford Nass, a professor at Stanford University, warned against the negative effect of multitasking. As he said in an interview:

"The research is almost unanimous, which is very rare in social science, and it says that people who chronically multitask show an enormous range of deficits. They're basically terrible at all sorts of cognitive tasks, including multitasking."

He continues:

"People who multitask all the time can't filter out irrelevancy. They can't manage a working memory. They're chronically distracted."

The bottom line is this. Multitasking doesn't work, and distractions kill your productivity. One of your most powerful assets is your ability to focus. Don't lose it by multitasking or allowing yourself to be distracted.

As mentioned previously, you don't need complicated techniques, systems or tools to boost your productivity. These will only have a marginal effect and tend to work only for people who are already very productive. What you need is:

1. To practice focusing completely on the task in front of you, and
2. To ensure this is a truly important task that moves the needle forward.

If you remember only one thing from this book, remember this:

One of the most effective ways to increase your productivity is to identify the correct tasks to work on and focus on them for at least forty-five minutes each day, while eliminating any distractions or interruptions.

Therefore, the first thing you need to do before anything else is to practice entering a deep state of concentration every day for forty-five minutes. Simply working on your major task, uninterrupted, for forty-five minutes each day *consistently* and without changing anything else in your routine, will significantly boost your productivity. Over time, and as you have more practice, you can add another forty-five-minute block of uninterrupted work, and then another one. This habit will become the foundation upon which you can build a more complex productivity system if needed.

In this part, you'll see in greater detail what you can specifically do to enter a state of flow and stay focused on your task.

1

THE BEST PRODUCTIVITY TOOL YOU'LL EVER HAVE

Do you want to know what your best productivity tool is? By now, you probably know.

It's your ability to focus.

Your focus is your superpower. It allows you to channel all your energy into one specific thing while excluding everything else. When you focus for long enough, you enter an altered state of mind, and you feel calmer and more in control. All your thoughts and worries disappear into the background, and you will be able to immerse yourself completely in the task in front of you. In this state of mind, you're far more effective and will end up achieving more.

Laser-shaper focus sustained over a long period of time can turn an average person into a genius—at least that's how this person will seem to others. This is because intense focus minimizes energy leakage by channeling energy towards the accomplishment of one specific thing. In short, it allows us to *invest* all our energy instead of squandering it.

Look around and you'll see many smart people misusing their talents. These people have no clear direction, they lack confidence and they have little discipline. As a result, they operate far below their true potential. On the other hand, you'll see many rather average people achieving extraordinary things and having a tremendous impact on society. A big part of this is due to their ability to stay focused over the long term. I would go as far as saying that extreme focus is like adding at least an extra twenty points to your IQ.

What about you? How good is your focus?

Learn to develop laser-sharp focus and most of your productivity challenges will vanish. Do it over a long enough period and you will be astonished by what you can accomplish.

Now, let's briefly cover one key principle you'll need to apply if you want to develop a laser-sharp focus.

The 80/20 Principle

This well-known rule states that twenty percent of your actions generate eighty percent of your results. In other words, only a fraction of what you do is truly effective. The idea is to spend as much time as possible on the twenty percent because that's what brings the biggest results.

For instance, I'm a full-time writer and guess what activity brings the most of my results?

That's correct—writing.

Every time I release a new book on Amazon, I receive a new boost of visibility. Each new book becomes another marketing tool that introduces thousands of new readers to my work. The more books I produce, the stronger my marketing power becomes. The second activity that brings a large part of my results is running ads on the Amazon platform.

Writing and running ads on Amazon are the two activities I spend the most of my effort on. On the other hand, promoting my books on social media or doing podcast interviews turned out to be a huge waste of time (at least for me). These days, I rarely engage in any of these activities.

What about you? What's the twenty percent of your activities that bring you eighty percent of your results? And what is the most important task you should be working on right now?

Before you can focus on your most important task fully and without interruption, you must know what that task is. Unfortunately, your key tasks may not be as simple as writing or running ads. Furthermore, they will likely change over time. This is why it's even more important for you to spend time identifying what these tasks may be.

To do so, make sure you:

- Internalize the 7-Step process introduced in the section "Approaching your tasks smartly",
- Research what blueprint others have used to reach a similar goal (and see if they could work for you), and
- Ask yourself smart questions such as, "If I could only work one day or one week and had to take a month off, what would I work on?" or "Is what I'm doing today moving me closer to where I want to be in five years?"

* * *

Action step

Using your action guide, identify the twenty percent of your activities that bring eighty percent of your results. Then, write them down.

2

DEVELOPING FOCUS

As we've just seen, your ability to laser-focus on one task at a time is key to enhancing your productivity. In this section, we're going to discuss how you can build your focus "muscle" and enter a state of flow more easily.

A. What is the "flow state"

The "flow state" is a mental state in which you're so fully immersed in an activity that you become hyper-focused, while experiencing a sense of underlying enjoyment. When you're in the flow state, you can become so absorbed by what you do that you lose track of time. According to the psychologist, Mihaly Csíkszentmihályi, author of *Flow*, such flow experiences are predicted to lead to positive affect as well as to better performance.

Jeanne Nakamura and Mihaly Csíkszentmihályi have identified six factors that characterize an experience of flow. In a state of flow:

- You're highly focused on the present moment,
- Your action and awareness fuse,
- You lose reflective self-consciousness (i.e., the ability you have to be aware of being aware),

- You feel in control of the situation or activity you're engaged in,
- Your experience of time is altered, and
- You find the activity intrinsically rewarding.

While these aspects can appear independently of each other, it's only in combination that they constitute a so-called flow experience as described by Mihaly Csíkszentmihályi.

When you're in the flow state, your focus is much deeper, your surroundings start fading away and any unrelated thoughts seem to disappear into the background. Negative thoughts may arise but since you don't give them any attention, they quickly vanish, enabling you to remain fully focused.

Now, it can take a little time before you enter the flow state, but the more engaged you are with a task—and the more concentration it requires—the more likely you are to experience such a state. Tackling jobs that are moderately challenging but not too challenging will also help. This is actually how many video games are designed. They hook players by implementing the right level of difficulty that will keep them engaged.

For me, such a state often occurs when I write or edit a book, since it requires a high level of focus.

What about you? When and how often do you experience the flow? And what are you doing specifically? Perhaps, more importantly, how could enter that state more often and at will?

When we think about it, the flow state is actually a natural thing. In absence of distractions, we tend to become absorbed in any tasks that require our full attention, whether it is writing, brainstorming new ideas or crafting a product. It is just that distractions have become omnipresent recently. To put it differently, focus is now a scarce commodity, while distraction has become the norm. Try staying away from social media, YouTube, Netflix, or any other source of distraction for three to six months and see what it does to your levels of focus.

According to the U.S. edition of the 2018 Global Mobile Consumer Survey from Deloitte, on average, people check their phones fifty-two times a day. To be honest, I suspect that, for many people, it is much more than that. One study conducted by researcher, Gloria Mark, also revealed that the average person checked their emails seventy-four times a day, with some people checking over four hundred times a day.

Under such circumstances, it is no wonder we struggle to remain focused. However, if you can regain (some) control over your ability to focus, you are likely to become one of the most productive people you know.

Now, let's discuss some specific things you can do to cultivate laser-sharp focus and enter a state of flow on a regular basis.

B. How to enter the flow state

a. Create daily routines

Creating routines is the most powerful way to sharpen your focus. When you build routines around the completion of your most important task(s), you start conditioning your mind. By performing a routine before beginning a work session, you'll make it easier to enter a deeper state of focus. The famous writer, Stephen King, writes every single morning, including Christmas day and his birthday. He doesn't wait for his creative muse to arrive. Instead, he demands that his muse manifests when it comes time to sit down and write. This is because he understands the following truth:

Inspiration seldom happens when we wait for it, it appears when we start taking action toward our goals.

The point is this. Don't wait for inspiration. Don't wait for the flow state to come to you. Work on *creating* that flow state. And it starts by putting in place a daily routine.

Now, let's see how to create your own routines.

How to create a daily routine

Your daily routine doesn't have to be complicated. Here are a few things that will help you build an effective routine.

1) **Be at the same place, at the same time every day.** This is pretty straightforward. For instance, these days, after taking a break from writing, I put in place a simple routine: I sit at my desk at the same time every morning. It helps me put myself in the right state of mind before work and it will do the same for you.

2) **Have a trigger to kickstart your routine.** You want to know when it's time to do your work. Having a specific trigger that signals the beginning of your routine will help. For instance, for me right now, it's a matter of drinking a glass of water, taking some vitamins and writing down my goals. As I'm going through this process, I make sure to take my time. This helps slow things down to facilitate the emergence of the flow state when I start writing.

You can also meditate for a few minutes or do some mindful exercises to make sure you are calm and present. (You can refer to previous exercises on mindfulness, meditation, and breathing for more on this topic.)

3) **Decide the type of work you'll do**

The next step is to determine what you will work on during your focused session. Identify your most important task—the one that is not only effective but also highly demanding. For me, it's writing. I can do a lot of busy work outside of writing, but if I don't write, I don't have a business.

What about you? What really moves the needle at work or in your personal life? Ideally, what you work on should be:

- **Demanding.** It should require a lot of your energy and attention to complete.
- **Challenging.** It should be difficult enough to engage you but not so hard that you give up or becoming overly frustrated.
- **Effective.** It should enable you to make progress toward an important professional or personal goal.

Note that it is often an activity you procrastinate on precisely because it's difficult and you doubt your ability to do it well.

4) Just start. Don't ponder on whether you can do a good job or not. And don't wait to feel as though you *can* do a good job, just begin. Remember, action creates motivation—it doesn't work as well the other way around. Therefore, give yourself permission to start working for just five minutes. Once you begin a task, you'll often build enough momentum to keep going.

Among other things, as part of your daily routine you can also:

- Meditate,
- Exercise,
- Stretch,
- Write down your goals,
- Write three things you're grateful for, and
- Visualize your goals.

5) Commit. The final step is to commit to doing your focused work. Commitment is critical since it will ensure you stay consistent and build a solid routine that will enhance your productivity.

I recommend you commit to your new daily routine for a minimum of thirty days. Inside your action guide, you'll find a thirty-day calendar you can use to hold yourself accountable. Remember, consistency is more important than intensity. Just doing one forty-five-minute session every day will, over time, significantly increase your focus and boost your productivity. This one daily session will have a ripple effect, enabling you to generate incredible momentum over time. When you've finished the first session, you might decide to continue and start a second session and a third. After that, you may begin to plan your day more meticulously. Just keep building momentum and see where it takes you.

b. Eliminate any distractions

The next thing you can do to enhance your focus is to remove all your distractions. In the next section we'll cover the different types of distractions and how to avoid them. But for now, turn off the notifications on your phone or computer and close all the unnecessary tabs. If you're at work, ask your colleagues/boss not to disturb you (if possible). You can also wear a set of headphones to signal to people you're working. If you're at home, tell your spouse, kids, parents or roommates to avoid disturbing you during this time. Remember that your focus is one of your biggest assets. It is your responsibility to protect it.

c. Work without interruptions

Now that you've removed distractions, work as intensely as you can during the block of time dedicated to your key task. As mentioned above, I recommend you start with a single forty-five-minute session. Do not stop before the end. Challenge yourself to stay focused. Over time, you'll become better and better at it.

According to Anders Eriksson, a psychologist at Florida State University who studied top performers in numerous fields, world-class performers usually don't do more than four hours of intense, deliberate work each day. Therefore, the ultimate end game would be for you to accomplish four hours of focused work each day (with breaks in-between). Sure, you might work longer if you are tackling fairly easy tasks, but you'll find it difficult to work more than four hours a day on highly demanding tasks. Experiment and see for yourself what works best for you.

* * *

Action step

Using the action guide, follow the steps above and create your own daily routine.

C. How to boost your ability to focus

a. Have something else to do other than work

If you find yourself being a workaholic, consider taking on a few hobbies. I know, if you're already busy this may sound counterintuitive, but unless you dedicate specific time each day or each week to your hobbies, you'll have little incentive to become more productive.

This advice is especially important if you're self-employed. Most self-employed people tend to work long hours. There are often no clear boundaries between their work and private life and the concept of weekends or vacations often disappears. You may be passionate about what you do, but it doesn't mean you should neglect your personal life and deny yourself weekends or vacations.

In his excellent book, *Deep Work*, Cal Newport described the concept of "fixed-schedule productivity". The idea is to set aside a specific amount of time for work each day before wrapping it up. Cal Newport rarely works after 5:30 pm. As he puts it, "A commitment to fixed-schedule productivity [...] shifts you into a scarcity mindset." When you adopt fixed-schedule productivity, suddenly, time becomes much more precious and you'll protect it more fiercely as a result.

Truth be told, I've been willing to implement such a schedule for over three years now, but I failed time and again. Each time, I would revert to doing busy and ineffective work in the evenings, often working seven days a week.

But I now understand why. It's because I didn't have enough activities outside of work. Having nothing scheduled after 6 pm, I would often end up working in the evenings. There's nothing wrong with running some ads at 10 pm or 11 pm, right?

As I mentioned previously, to solve that issue, I sat down and wrote all the exciting things I could be doing after work each day. I reconnected with my goals of learning languages and studying various topics, and I ended up adding the following activities to my schedules:

- Estonian study (every day),
- Japanese study (every day),
- Economics course online (two or three times a week), and
- "Learn how to learn" online course (twice a week).

In fact, working long hours usually doesn't work. According to a study published in 2014 by John Pencavel of Stanford University, employees' productivity falls significantly when they work over fifty hours a week, and even more dramatically when they work over fifty-five hours. More interestingly, it shows that someone who puts in seventy hours produces nothing more with those extra fifteen hours. Now, you may need to work long hours occasionally but make sure it doesn't become a habit. Forty hours of solid work every week should be more than enough.

In 2017, another study conducted by Voucher Cloud—a major UK money-saving brand—revealed that the average UK office worker is productive for only two hours and fifty-three minutes each day (or about one third of the time spent at the office). And this is likely to be the same for workers all over the world.

Personal development blogger, Steve Pavlina, came to a similar conclusion as he wrote in his article *Triple Your Personal Productivity*. He kept a personal time log for a week, writing down every work-related task. At the end of the week, he realized that, while he spent sixty hours at the office, he did only fifteen hours' worth of actual work. He then practiced doing real work only. He found that his optimal limit was forty-five hours per week.

The bottom line is that you should adopt a fixed-schedule productivity system and avoid working long hours. Find one or two exciting hobbies you've always wanted to try and add them to your after-work schedule. It will make you more productive. Then, when you're at work, don't mess about, work!

Additional tips:

Alternatively, try shortening your working day if you can (If you're self-employed for instance). For the next seven days, give yourself only four or five hours to work each day and see how it impacts your productivity. Usually, the less time you have, the more likely you are to use it productively.

b. Read

Reading is an effective way to increase your concentration since it is an active process as opposed to watching TV or listening to podcasts, which is much more passive. Therefore, try reading more and for longer periods of time each day.

c. Allow yourself to be bored

These days, we're constantly overstimulated. What do you do when you find yourself waiting in a queue? If you're like most people, you immediately take out your phone and start checking Facebook, Instagram or your emails (or darn it, you might even make a phone call!). The problem is that, when you're continuously stimulated, simple activities seem boring, while important tasks become unappealing.

Studies have shown that when we let a rat stimulate its medial forebrain bundle (a group of dopamine axons), it will do so thousands of times an hour forgoing even eating. These studies demonstrate that every activity that triggers dopamine release can make us want more of the same. This is why we often find it so hard to stop checking our phones. For this reason, dopamine is sometimes referred to as the "molecule of more".

Therefore, if you find yourself being overstimulated, practice being bored and doing nothing. Go for a walk in the countryside or your local city park. Stop checking your phone for a day. Or eat in silence. As you reduce external stimuli, the difficult tasks you've been putting off will become more appealing. By being less stimulated, you'll get a greater kick out of working on these tasks and focusing on them will come more easily.

People think I'm naturally disciplined. It may be partially true, but I'm also easily distracted. If I start checking my book sales or talking with friends on Facebook, I become completely restless and find myself looking for more and more stimulation. Demanding activities like writing become almost impossible to engage in. On the other hand, when I start my day with little to no stimulation, relax my mind and begin to write, it becomes far easier to start writing.

To conclude, being bored is healthy. Consequently, you should lower your level of stimulation by eliminating highly stimulating activities such as checking social media or playing video games. This will make it easier for you to tackle your most important tasks and remain focused.

d. Batch unimportant work

By batching (or grouping) minor jobs, you can free time to focus on your core tasks. You can also batch highly stimulating tasks as a way to lower your overall level of stimulation. For instance, you could limit yourself to thirty to sixty minutes each day to check your emails and social media. Doing so will prevent you from checking them compulsively throughout the day.

f. Take breaks

If we allow ourselves to become caught up in the busyness of our days, we often neglect to take breaks. The logic is, we can work longer and accomplish more—or so we think. However, productivity isn't just about time. It's about the intensity and level of intentionality we put into the time we have. By not taking breaks, we're usually being less intentional. Working without interruption also depletes our energy faster, leading to suboptimal productivity.

Imagine the following two cases.

In one case, you work without breaks, jumping from one task to the next throughout your day.

In the other case, you plan your day meticulously, you know exactly what you have to do, and you take breaks between each work session to refresh yourself and prepare yourself to work on the next task.

In which case do you think you'll be the most productive?

Therefore, practice taking breaks regularly and be more intentional with the way you use your time and energy. It will make you much more effective overall.

* * *

Action step

Using your action guide, write down at least one specific thing you will do to sharpen your focus.

g. Practice focusing anytime and anywhere

In his book, *Deep Work*, Cal Newport identifies four different philosophies when it comes to focusing on our work. One of them is what he called the "Journalistic Philosophy". The idea behind this philosophy is to use small chunks of time during your day to practice focused work (similar to the way journalists meet the incessant deadlines their job requires).

If you want to develop your focus, practice working anytime anywhere until it becomes a habit. For instance, perhaps you can work on the train. Or, perhaps you can work while queueing. Some writers managed to write entire books on their phones while on the train during their daily commute to and from work! And writing isn't necessarily the easiest thing to do, considering how many writers experience mental blocks.

The point is, you can learn to enter a focused state more quickly. And the more you practice, the easier it will become. Once you're able to work almost anywhere anytime, you will have a superpower very few people ever acquire.

Additional tip:

During these impromptu work sessions, you can repeat parts of the routine you use to enter the flow state each morning. For instance, you could listen to the same music you listen to during your daily routine.

* * *

Action step

Using your action guide, answer the following question:

During what specific moments or activities could I practice focusing, even if it's just for five minutes?

h. Never feel guilty

My last tip in this section is to avoid feeling guilty if your work session isn't as productive as you'd intended. Some days are better and more productive than others. But the more you practice developing focus, the better you will become at it.

Blaming yourself doesn't work. Instead, practice being self-compassionate. Self-compassion is one of the most powerful tools you can use to improve your productivity. The more you're able to encourage yourself, the better your emotional state will become. Furthermore, the better you feel, the more you will be compelled to take action toward your goals. Self-compassion is especially powerful when you start feeling a little depressed. It is what I call "a safety net to our emotional well-being". Make sure you use this safety net to protect yourself.

Personally, I started practicing self-compassion a little over three years ago. It allowed me to feel better about myself during challenging times, and it helped me to reach many of my goals. So, if you believe you must be harsh on yourself to prevent you from becoming complacent, don't worry. You can be both self-compassionate and accomplish a great deal. Try it and see how well it works.

Now, let me give you a few simple tips you can use to cultivate self-compassion.

- Stop berating yourself. Whenever you notice you're putting yourself down, stop and reformulate your thoughts. For instance, if you called yourself stupid, say to yourself, "It's okay to make mistakes. Everyone does. I'll be more careful next time."
- Undertake a 7-day self-compassion challenge. For the next seven days, monitor your internal self-talk and try to be as nice to yourself as possible. Notice how your inner dialogue impacts your mood both positively and negatively.
- Let go of the following disempowering myths about self-compassion. The first myth is the idea you need to be hard on yourself to get anything done. The second is that self-compassion is for weak-minded people. And the third is that self-compassion is selfish. In truth, when you treat yourself well, you'll achieve more, become tougher, and be in a better place emotionally to help others.

Therefore, be nice to yourself. You'll be more motivated and will accomplish more over the long term.

In conclusion, to enter the flow state more easily you must:

- Create a daily routine to put yourself in the right state of mind before work,
- Get started for at least five minutes (action generates motivation),
- Eliminate distractions so that you can stay focused on your work, and
- Practice working without interruption to build your focus muscle.

To make it even easier to focus:

- Allow yourself to be bored to lower your stimulation level and tackle difficult and unappealing tasks more easily,
- Read more to develop your concentration,

- Batch minor tasks to free time to focus on your most important work,
- Take breaks frequently and deliberately to recharge your battery and increase your focus,
- Practice deep work whenever you have a few minutes during the day, and
- Never feel guilty but be self-compassionate instead.

3

ELIMINATING DISTRACTIONS

In today's world, it has never been easier to become distracted. After all, we are just one click away from all the knowledge in the world, but also from all the distractions we can ever imagine. In one click, you can connect to Facebook and see what your friends are up to. You can check your emails and see if there is any exciting news. Or you can go on YouTube and watch just one video before going back to work—or so you tell yourself.

In other words, distractions are everywhere, and we can easily allow ourselves to be tempted. This is especially true when we're supposed to be working on a challenging, boring or unpleasant task.

Eliminating distractions is one of the most important things you can do to regain control over your time. It will allow you to focus one hundred percent on the task at hand and channel your energy toward its completion.

Now, let's see how you can start creating a distraction-free environment.

A. The distraction matrix and how to work distraction-free

In this section, I'll share a simple framework to illustrate a number of different types of distractions and the problems each creates.

During your day you can be distracted in four main different ways. That is, you can be:

1. Dragged,
2. Interrupted,
3. Seduced, and
4. Fooled.

1) Being dragged

Have you ever wasted thirty minutes checking your Facebook newsfeed after you opened the app just to check one message? Have you ever spent an hour reading and responding to emails while you only wanted to reply to one specific email?

I certainly have.

In these cases, you've been dragged. Being dragged simply means having the intention of doing something and while doing it, being pulled in another direction and wasting a load of time as a result. Now, this is nothing to be ashamed of—we all do the same thing during the day. The key to avoiding these types of distractions is to become more aware of what they are.

For instance, I know that for me, Facebook and YouTube have an extremely strong pulling power and will take me with them if I'm not careful.

To avoid being dragged into the abyss of time-wasting, look at all the distractions you have during your day and identify which ones have the greatest pulling power. Perhaps it is talking with a colleague. Perhaps it is checking the news. Or perhaps it is going on Twitter. Once you've identified these strongest pulls, you can start creating a strategy to stay away from them. To protect yourself against the pull, here is the key question to ask:

Is this activity likely to derail me?

If so, you know you're walking into a minefield. You will be better off scheduling time for that activity later during the day or removing it from your life altogether.

2) Being interrupted

As we learned earlier, a study conducted by Gloria Mark from the University of California, discovered that, on average, every employee spends a mere eleven minutes on a given project before being interrupted.

What about you? How often are you interrupted during your day? Interruptions don't have the same pulling power as the distractions we discussed above, but they tend to occur more often during the working day. If you let them, interruptions will kill your focus and prevent you from entering a deep state of concentration.

Examples of such interruptions are:

- Notifications on your phone or computers,
- Colleagues talking to you, and
- Phone calls.

Note that these interruptions don't have to be external. You can interrupt your work yourself, and you often do. This is the case when you check Facebook, read an article online or check your phone. Such interruptions usually happen for a couple of reasons:

- They have become unconscious habits. For example, every time you check notifications or check your phone expecting to see one, you get a dopamine hit. As you repeat this action over and over again, it becomes a habit.
- Interruptions can act as a coping mechanism to avoid work. Whenever you need to work on a boring, challenging or unpleasant task, you'll often feel the sudden urge to distract yourself. In a sense, this is a mental "runaway" from the situation.

The key questions you can ask when you're being interrupted or when you interrupt yourself are:

Is this killing my ability to focus?

Is this preventing me from entering a deep state of concentration?

If so, what can I do about it?

3) Being seduced

Have you ever abandoned your work to focus on something that looks more exciting? Or have you ever put off an important task to work on something easier?

This is what I refer to as "being seduced".

Whenever you engage in this type of behavior, you're looking for something that will make you feel good. You choose fairly easy tasks to check these items off your to-do list and feel good about yourself. However, completing a number of inconsequential tasks has little to do with being productive. It doesn't say anything about how well you're using your time.

Many people engage in feel-good activities to keep themselves busy and maintain the illusion they're working, but this is just being busy. Feel-good activities often distract you from doing meaningful work. They can be simple tasks, but they can also be bigger projects that consume your time while failing to move you closer to your goals.

Feel-good activities are often the opposite of meaningful activities. They may give you a shot of dopamine, but the pleasant feeling will be short-lived. Conversely, when you learn to focus on completing difficult and meaningful work instead, you'll develop a healthier sense of self-esteem that will stay with you much longer.

Feel-good activities can, however, be effective in building momentum and getting you unstuck. As such, they shouldn't be dismissed completely. For instance, when you feel unmotivated, it might be a good idea to complete a list of small tasks to rebuild your motivation. To learn how to maintain a healthy level of motivation in greater depth, please refer to Book 2 in the Mastery Series, *Master Your Motivation*.

To help you avoid this type of distraction, the key questions you can ask yourself are:

- Is this activity really what I should be doing *right now*?
- Am I tackling this task just to keep myself busy and feel good or because it's truly important?

4) Being fooled

Have you read dozens of books on productivity to figure out how to design the ultimate productivity system? Do you keep trying new tools or apps, hoping to find the perfect one for you?

We often distract ourselves from doing the hard work by looking for the next productivity app, book or course. We tell ourselves that if only we could find the right tool, we'll finally be able to reach maximum productivity and achieve anything we desire. However, this is an illusion. Some of the most productive people on earth lived centuries ago and had none of the productivity tools we have today. They had no phones and no internet to search for information. Think of Benjamin Franklin or Leonardo da Vinci for instance. If anything, technology is a major distraction that prevents us from entering a deeper level of focus and getting real work done.

Put another way, "being fooled" means believing there is a magic pill out there that will solve all your productivity problems. It means trying new techniques over and over while failing to understand the fundamentals of productivity. It's thinking you need to keep adding more stuff to your system.

More specifically, you fool yourself when your productivity system isn't simple enough to be sustained over the long term. Unless you have a sustainable system that works for you, you'll struggle to maintain a high level of productivity. As we discussed earlier, if you try to implement a system that is currently out of your reach (i.e., unrealistic for you), you'll set yourself up for failure. As a result, you'll give up and look for another system, and you will end up repeating the cycle over and over.

The point is, there is no magic pill to turn you into a productivity machine overnight. In my opinion, the closest thing to a magic pill, is to practice developing unshakeable focus by working on your most important task without interruption for at least forty-five minutes a day—and to improve your ability to focus over time. Benjamin Franklin and Leonardo da Vinci weren't interrupted by phone notifications. They weren't tempted to scroll through social media. Nor did they have the option to binge-watch TV series either. With fewer distractions, they likely had an easier time staying focused. As a result, even though they didn't have access to today's technological tools, they could achieve far more than most people today.

Remember, with laser-sharp focus sustained over a long period of time, you can achieve almost anything you desire. Once you have developed the ability to focus deeply, you can begin to add productivity blocks on top of it such as more advanced planning or enhanced accountability. (For more on this, refer to **Part I. Understanding Productivity** — section 3. The five levels of productivity.)

To avoid being fooled, the key questions to ask yourself are:

- Am I still looking for more information on being more productive instead of applying the fundamentals?
- Is my productivity system sustainable over the long term or is it too big of a stretch?
- If it's the latter, what can I do about it?

* * *

Action step

Using your action guide, write down all the ways you're being dragged, interrupted, seduced and fooled. Refer to the following grid.

1. Dragged	2. Interrupted
Q: Is this activity likely to derail me?	Q: Is this hampering my activity to do focused work?
3. Seduced	**4. Fooled**
Q: Is this activity really what I should be doing now?	Q: Am I still looking for fancy productivity tools? Is my current system sustainable over the long term?

B. Identify your biggest distraction

We've previously seen that there are four types of distractions robbing you of your ability to focus. You can be:

- Dragged by activities that derail you,
- Interrupted multiples times, which destroys your focus,
- Seduced by feel-good activities that keep you away from your key tasks, and
- Fooled by complex systems or tools that fail to improve your productivity.

Now, I would like you to think of the one activity that has the biggest distraction power. This is what Jake Knapp and John Zeratsky call your "Kryptonite" in their book *Make Time*. To identify it, ask yourself the following question:

If you could eliminate just one distraction, which one would have the biggest positive impact on your ability to focus?

For instance, the biggest distraction for me is YouTube. If I'm not careful, I can spend hours on it. While doing so may be entertaining, it doesn't move me closer to my goals. Nor does it create lasting fulfillment. Whenever I cut back on YouTube, my motivation increases and my productivity soars.

What about you? What is your number one biggest distraction?

* * *

Action step

Using your action guide, complete the exercises below:

- Make a list of the distractions you're a victim of for each type (dragged, interrupted, seduced and fooled).
- Underline the ones you tend to waste the most time on.
- Identify the one activity with the biggest power to distract you and create a plan to eliminate it or reduce its impact.

C. CEO/COO/employee framework

The four types of distractions can be avoided when you learn how to take better control of your day. This includes planning effectively. In this section, we're going to explore a framework I call CEO/COO/employee. I first heard about it from the Doctor and YouTuber, Ali Abidaal (though he uses the roles pilot, airplane and engineer instead).

Put simply, you can play three different roles during the day:

- CEO,
- COO, and
- Employee.

Now, let's see what each title stands for.

The CEO:

The CEO (Chief Executive Officer) sets the agenda for the day. As the CEO, you decide what must be done based on the big picture strategy you have already established. You ensure that the employee is doing their job during the day. To help the employee be as effective as possible, you must make sure that the employee:

- Knows *what* to do, so that they can start working right away,
- Knows *how* to do it, so that they can complete their task effectively, and
- Knows *why* they must do it, so that they have the motivation needed to see the task through.

Now, the key point when you use this framework is to avoid switching roles during the day. In other words, once you (the CEO) set the strategy for the day, your job is done, and you shouldn't be disturbed after that. The employee should then focus single-mindedly on the task in front of them, knowing it will improve their life/career.

The COO:

The COO (Chief Operations Officer) is in charge of improving the system alongside the CEO. For instance, as the COO, you can install daily routines or improve the way the employee works on a specific task.

As the COO you support the employee by:

- Identifying the most effective way for them to approach the tasks,
- Brainstorming ideas and making suggestions to help them improve your productivity
- Putting in place daily routines, and

Finally, you report your findings to the CEO so that they can plan the day better.

The Employee:

When you are the employee, your role is simply to tackle your tasks, one at a time and with ruthless focus. The main benefits are that you don't need to:

- Overthink things, which is the job of the CEO (an employee's role is to execute),
- Hesitate (simply do what you were told to do unless there is an emergency), or
- Feel motivated. (Motivation comes and goes. If the CEO did a good job, you should be somewhat motivated because you understand that all the tasks you're tackling move you closer to your goals.)

Also, remember all the long-term benefits you'll gain from trusting the CEO. By following their instructions every day, you'll become more productive and will achieve far more than you otherwise would. Such is the power of using this framework. Let the CEO think and strategize and let the employee act and complete the work.

This framework is simpler than it looks. In a nutshell, the CEO plans the day, the COO looks for ways to improve the system, and the employee executes without overthinking.

Now, let's give a couple of examples to help you understand the system better.

For instance, as a CEO, I've decided that I will write from 9 am to noon today. As an employee, the only thing I need to do this morning is to sit at my desk and start typing (which is what I'm doing right now). As a COO, I will assess how well I performed that task. What I noticed (as the COO) is that, to write three hours a day (with breaks every forty-five minutes or so), I need to have a decent outline and specific ideas of what I'll be writing about. As a result, the COO could suggest the CEO spends more time working on the outline. That way, the employee will have an easier time writing each day.

Let's consider another example. Imagine you, as the CEO, decided that today you will work on a specific project for two hours. As an employee, you immediately start working on this project but after two hours have only completed fifty percent of the task. You will then tell the COO about it. The COO may decide that, moving forward, the CEO should give the employee more time to complete similar tasks. Or the COO may identify what has prevented the employee from completing the task. Perhaps the employee needs to upgrade a skill that acts as a bottleneck. Perhaps the employee could have approached it differently. Or perhaps the employee could have asked someone for help and delegated part of the task.

Ultimately, you're the CEO of your own life. When you plan your day and execute consistently, you take control of your destiny and make the achievement of many of your goals much more likely.

* * *

Action step

Using your action guide, practice asking yourself the following questions at the start of each day:

CEO:

- Exactly what tasks do I need to complete today?

Employee:

- Do I know how to do the tasks?
- Do I have the skills/tools to complete them?
- Do I know why I need to do these tasks?
- Am I on board?
- Am I committed to doing them?
- If I feel inner resistance, what can I do to overcome it?

COO:

- What did I do well today?
- What could I have done better?
- What could be improved and exactly how?

Then, take a pen and piece of paper and write down the three main tasks you'd like to complete today and begin to work.

CONCLUSION

I hope that this book offered you a valuable opportunity to reflect on the way you're currently using your time. We all know that our time is precious, but we don't always use it effectively to achieve our exciting goals. If we aren't careful, over our lifetime, we can easily waste not just hundreds, but thousands of hours engaging in unproductive activities.

When stuck in the same old routine, we can end up abandoning our goals and settling for less than we're truly capable of achieving. We keep saying we don't have time without asking ourselves how we could *make* the time.

But you now understand it doesn't have to be this way.

By studying how you use your time, and by redirecting your focus toward the right activities, you can regain control over your time and use this invaluable asset to design a better future.

Therefore, instead of complaining you don't have enough time, why not ask yourself, "What am I going to do with the very little time I have available to me?"

So, how are you going to use the precious asset that even the richest people on earth like Warren Buffet, Elon Musk and Bill Gates are unable to buy more of?

I will leave you with this thought.

Remember, at any time, what you do is either:

- Meaningful, enjoyable and/or moves you closer to your goals, or
- Devoid of meaning, boring and/or moves you further away from them.

Therefore, stay focused on your main goals and make progress toward them each and every day. Time will pass anyway, so you might as well use it in a meaningful way.

I wish you all the best with the precious time you've been given.
Warm regards,
Thibaut

What do you think?

I hope you benefit from this book. I would be very grateful if you could take a moment to leave an honest review on Amazon.

Thanks again for your support!

Thibaut

MASTER YOUR EMOTIONS (PREVIEW)

 The mind is its own place, and in itself can make a heaven of Hell, a hell of Heaven.

— JOHN MILTON, POET.

We all experience a wide range of emotions throughout our lives. I had to admit, while writing this book, I experienced highs and lows myself. At first, I was filled with excitement and thrilled at the idea of providing people with a guide to help them understand their emotions. I imagined how readers' lives would improve as they learned to control their emotions. My motivation was high and I couldn't help but imagine how great the book would be.

Or so I thought.

After the initial excitement, the time came to sit down to write the actual book, and that's when the excitement wore off pretty quickly. Suddenly ideas that looked great in my mind felt dull. My writing seemed boring, and I felt as though I had nothing substantive or valuable to contribute.

Sitting at my desk and writing became more challenging each day. I started losing confidence. Who was I to write a book about emotions if I couldn't even master my own emotions? How ironic! I considered giving up. There are already plenty of books on the topic, so why add one more?

At the same time, I realized this book was a perfect opportunity to work on my emotional issues. And who doesn't suffer from negative emotions from time to time? We all have highs and lows, don't we? The key is what we *do* with our lows. Are we using our emotions to grow and learn or are we beating ourselves up over them?

So, let's talk about *your* emotions now. Let me start by asking you this:

How do you feel right now?

Knowing how you feel is the first step toward taking control of your emotions. You may have spent so much time internalizing you've lost touch with your feelings. Perhaps you answered as follows: "I feel this book could be useful," or "I really feel I could learn something from this book."

However, none of these answers reflect on how you feel. You don't 'feel like this,' or 'feel like that,' you simply 'feel.' You don't 'feel like' this book could be useful, you 'think' this book could be useful, and that generates an emotion which makes you 'feel' excited about reading it. Feelings manifest as physical sensations in your body, not as an idea in your mind. Perhaps, the reason the word 'feel' is so often overused or misused is because we don't want to talk about our emotions.

So, how do you feel now?

Why is it important to talk about emotions?

How you feel determines the quality of your life. Your emotions can make your life miserable or truly magical. That's why they are among the most essential things on which to focus. Your emotions color all your experiences. When you feel good, everything seems, feels, or tastes better. You also think better thoughts. Your energy levels are higher and possibilities seem limitless. Conversely, when you feel depressed, everything seems dull. You have little energy and you become unmotivated. You feel stuck in a place (mentally and physically) you don't want to be, and the future looks gloomy.

Your emotions can also act as a powerful guide. They can tell you something is wrong and allow you to make changes in your life. As such, they may be among the most powerful personal growth tools you have.

Sadly, neither your teachers nor your parents taught you how emotions work or how to control them. I find it ironic that just about anything comes with a how-to manual, while your mind doesn't. You've never received an instruction manual to teach you how your mind works and how to use it to better manage your emotions, have you? I haven't. In fact, until now, I doubt one even existed.

What you'll learn in this book

This book is the how-to manual your parents should have given you at birth. It's the instruction manual you should have received at school. In it, I'll share everything you need to know about emotions so you can overcome your fears and limitations and become the type of person you want to be.

More specifically, this book will help you:

- Understand what emotions are and how they impact your life
- Understand how emotions form and how you can use them for your personal growth
- Identify negative emotions that control your life and learn to overcome them
- Change your story to take better control over your life and create a more compelling future,
- Reprogram your mind to experience more positive emotions.
- Deal with negative emotions and condition your mind to create more positive ones

- Gain all the tools you need to start recognizing and controlling your emotions

Here is a more detailed summary of what you'll learn in this book:

In **Part I**, we'll discuss what emotions are. You'll learn why your brain is wired to focus on negativity and what you can do to counter this effect. You'll also discover how your beliefs impinge upon your emotions. Finally, you'll learn how negative emotions work and why they are so tricky.

In **Part II**, we'll go over the things that directly impact your emotions. You'll understand the roles your body, your thoughts, your words, or your sleep, play in your life and how you can use them to change your emotions.

In **Part III**, you'll learn how emotions form and how to condition your mind to experience more positive emotions.

And finally, in **Part IV**, we'll discuss how to use your emotions as a tool for personal growth. You'll learn why you experience emotions such as fear or depression and how they work.

Let's get started.

To start mastering your emotions today go to

mybook.to/Master_Emotions

I. What emotions are

Have you ever wondered what emotions are and what purpose they serve?

In this section, we'll discuss how your survival mechanism affects your emotions. Then, we'll explain what the 'ego' is and how it impacts your emotions. Finally, we'll discover the mechanism behind emotions and learn why it can be so hard to deal with negative ones.

Why people have a bias towards negativity

Your brain is designed for survival, which explains why you're able to read this book at this very moment. When you think about it, the probability of you being born was extremely low. For this miracle to happen, all the generations before you had to survive long enough to procreate. In their quest for survival and procreation, they must have faced death hundreds or perhaps thousands of times.

Fortunately, unlike your ancestors, you're (probably) not facing death every day. In fact, in many parts of the world, life has never been safer. Yet, your survival mechanism hasn't changed much. Your brain still scans your environment looking for potential threats.

In many ways, some parts of your brain have become obsolete. While you may not be seconds away from being eaten by a predator, your brain still gives significantly more weight to adverse events than to positive ones.

Fear of rejection is one example of a bias toward negativity. In the past, being rejected by your tribe would reduce your chances of survival significantly. Therefore, you learned to look for any sign of rejection, and this became hardwired in your brain.

Nowadays, being rejected often carries little or no consequence to your long-term survival. You can be hated by the entire world and still have a job, a roof and plenty of food on the table, yet, your brain remains programmed to perceive rejection as a threat to your survival.

This hardwiring is why rejection can be so painful. While you know most rejections are no big deal, you nevertheless feel the emotional pain. If you listen to your mind, you may even create a whole drama around it. You may believe you aren't worthy of love and dwell on a rejection for days or weeks. Worse still, you may become depressed as a result of this rejection.

One single criticism can often outweigh hundreds of positive ones. That's why, an author with fifty 5-star reviews, is likely to feel terrible when they receive a single 1-star review. While the author understands the 1-star review isn't a threat to her survival, her authorial brain doesn't. It likely interprets the negative review as a threat to her ego which triggers an emotional reaction.

The fear of rejection can also lead you to over-dramatize events. If your boss criticized you at work, your brain might see the criticism as a threat and you now think, "What if my boss fires me? What if I can't find a job quickly enough and my wife leaves me? What about my kids? What if I can't see them again?"

While you are fortunate to have such a useful survival mechanism, it is also your responsibility to separate real threats from imaginary ones. If you don't, you'll experience unnecessary pain and worry that will negatively impact the quality of your life. To overcome this bias towards negativity, you must reprogram your mind. One of a human being's greatest powers is our ability to use our thoughts to shape our reality and interpret events in a more empowering way. This book will teach you how to do this.

Why your brain's job isn't to make you happy

Your brain's primary responsibility is not to make you happy, but to ensure your survival. Thus, if you want to be happy, you must actively take control of your emotions rather than hoping you'll be happy because it's your natural state. In the following section, we'll discuss what happiness is and how it works.

How dopamine can mess with your happiness

Dopamine is a neurotransmitter that, among other functions, plays a significant role in rewarding certain behaviors. When dopamine releases into specific areas of your brain—the pleasure centers—you get an intense sense of wellbeing similar to a high. This sense of wellbeing is what happens during exercise, when you gamble, have sex, or eat great food.

One of the roles of dopamine is to ensure you look for food so you don't die of starvation, and you search for a mate so you can reproduce. Without dopamine, our species would likely be extinct by now. It's a pretty good thing, right?

Well, yes and no. In today's world, this reward system is, in many cases, obsolete. In the past, dopamine directly linked to our survival, now, it can be stimulated artificially. A great example of this effect is social media, which uses psychology to suck as much time as possible out of your life. Have you noticed all these notifications that pop up regularly? They're used to trigger a release of dopamine so you stay connected, and the longer you stay connected, the more money the services make. Watching pornography or gambling also leads to a release of dopamine which can make these activities highly addictive.

Fortunately, we don't need to act each time our brain releases dopamine. For instance, we don't need to continuously check our Facebook newsfeeds just because it gives us a pleasurable shot of dopamine.

Today's society is selling a version of happiness that can make us *un*happy. We've become addicted to dopamine mainly because of marketers who have found effective ways to exploit our brains. We receive multiple shots of dopamine throughout the day and we love it. But is that the same thing as happiness?

Worse than that, dopamine can create real addictions with severe consequences on our health. Research conducted at Tulane University showed that, when permitted to self-stimulate their pleasure center, participants did it an average of forty times per minute. They chose the stimulation of their pleasure center over food, even refusing to eat when hungry!

Korean, Lee Seung Seop is an extreme case of this syndrome. In 2005, Mr Seop died after playing a video game for fifty-eight hours straight with very little food or water, and no sleep. The subsequent investigation concluded the cause of death was heart failure induced by exhaustion and dehydration. He was only twenty-eight years old.

To take control of your emotions, you must understand the role dopamine plays and how it affects your happiness. Are you addicted to your phone? Are you glued to your TV? Or maybe you spend too much time playing video games. Most of us are addicted to something. For some people it's obvious, but for others, it's more subtle. For instance, you could be addicted to thinking. To better control your emotions, you must recognize and shed the light on your addictions as they can rob you of your happiness.

The 'one day I will' myth

Do you believe that one day you will achieve your dream and finally be happy? It is unlikely to happen. You may (and I hope you will) achieve your goal, but you won't live 'happily ever after.' This thinking is just another trick your mind plays on you.

Your mind quickly acclimates to new situations, which is probably the result of evolution and our need to adapt continually to survive and reproduce. This acclimatization is also probably why the new car or house you want will only make you happy for a while. Once the initial excitement wears off, you'll move on to crave the next exciting thing. This phenomenon is known as 'hedonic adaptation.'

How hedonic adaptation works

Let me share an interesting study that will likely change the way you see happiness. This study, which was conducted in 1978 on lottery winners and paraplegics, was incredibly eye-opening for me. The investigation evaluated how winning the lottery or becoming a paraplegic influence happiness:

The study found that one year after the event, both groups were just as happy as they were beforehand. Yes, just as happy (or unhappy). You can find more about it by watching Dan Gilbert's TED Talk, The Surprising Science of Happiness.

Perhaps you believe that you'll be happy once you've 'made it.' But, as the above study on happiness shows, this is simply not true. No matter what happens to you, your mind works by reverting to your predetermined level of happiness once you've adapted to the new event.

Does that mean you can't be happier than you are right now? No. What it means is that, in the long run, external events have minimal impact on your level of happiness.

In fact, according to Sonja Lyubomirsky, author of *The How of Happiness*, fifty percent of our happiness is determined by genetics, forty percent by internal factors, and only ten percent by external factors. These external factors include such things as whether we're single or married, rich or poor, and similar social influences.

The influence of external factors is probably way less than you thought. The bottom line is this: Your attitude towards life influences your happiness, not what happens to you.

By now, you understand how your survival mechanism negatively impacts your emotions and prevents you from experiencing more joy and happiness in your life. In the next section, we'll learn about the ego.

To read more visit my author page at:

amazon.com/author/thibautmeurisse

OTHER BOOKS BY THE AUTHORS:

Crush Your Limits: Break Free from Limitations and Achieve Your True Potential

Goal Setting: The Ultimate Guide to Achieving Life-Changing Goals

Habits That Stick: The Ultimate Guide to Building Habits That Stick Once and For All

Master Your Beliefs: A Practical Guide to Stop Doubting Yourself and Build Unshakeable Confidence

Master Your Destiny: A Practical Guide to Rewrite Your Story and Become the Person You Want to Be

Master Your Emotions: A Practical Guide to Overcome Negativity and Better Manage Your Feelings

Master Your Focus: A Practical Guide to Stop Chasing the Next Thing and Focus on What Matters Until It's Done

Master Your Motivation: A Practical Guide to Unstick Yourself, Build Momentum and Sustain Long-Term Motivation

Master Your Success: Timeless Principles to Develop Inner Confidence and Create Authentic Success

Master Your Thinking: A Practical Guide to Align Yourself with Reality and Achieve Tangible Results in the Real World

Productivity Beast: An Unconventional Guide to Getting Things Done

The Greatness Manifesto: Overcome Your Fear and Go After What You Really Want

The One Goal: Master the Art of Goal Setting, Win Your Inner Battles, and Achieve Exceptional Results

The Passion Manifesto: Escape the Rat Race, Uncover Your Passion and Design a Career and Life You Love

The Thriving Introvert: Embrace the Gift of Introversion and Live the Life You Were Meant to Live

The Ultimate Goal Setting Planner: Become an Unstoppable Goal

Achiever in 90 Days or Less

Upgrade Yourself: Simple Strategies to Transform Your Mindset, Improve Your Habits and Change Your Life

Success is Inevitable: 17 Laws to Unlock Your Hidden Potential, Skyrocket Your Confidence and Get What You Want From Life

Wake Up Call: How To Take Control Of Your Morning And Transform Your Life

ABOUT THE AUTHOR

THIBAUT MEURISSE

Thibaut Meurisse is a personal development blogger, author, and founder of whatispersonaldevelopment.org. M

Obsessed with self-improvement and fascinated by the power of the brain, his personal mission is to help people realize their full potential and reach higher levels of fulfillment and consciousness.

In love with foreign languages, he is French, writes in English, and lived in Japan for almost ten years.

Learn more about Thibaut at:

amazon.com/author/thibautmeurisse
whatispersonaldevelopment.org
thibaut.meurisse@gmail.com

Step-by-Step
Workbook

PART I. UNDERSTANDING PRODUCTIVITY

1. The importance of meaning

Are you making a meaningful use of your time right now?

For each statement below, rate yourself on the scale from 1 to 10 (one being false, ten being true). Be honest! You're doing this for you.

I find the time I spend at my work meaningful:

0 _____ 10

I'm using my personal time in a meaningful way:

0 _____ 10

I'm having meaningful relationships (friendships and/or intimate relationships):

0 _____ 10

Write down what you'd like to change below (if anything)

2. Productivity isn't only about time management

Answer the following statements:

I make the most of my peak hours each day.

0 _____ 10

I work on each task with focus while eliminated distractions.

0 _____ 10

The tasks I work on usually move me closer to my long-term goals.

0 _____ 10

I'm excited about most of the tasks I'm working on.

0 _____ 10

The Energy Cycle and its Six Phases

Your productivity level depends on your energy level and how effectively you can channel your energy towards activities that matter. Remember the six phases below:

1. Protect energy. Your energy is limited, and the best way to protect it is to increase the quality of your sleep, eat more healthily, and exercise more regularly. When you fail to do so, your available energy decreases.

2. Channel energy. Energy that is not directed toward a specific purpose will dissipate and be of little value. Once that energy dissipates, you'll *never* be able to get it back. Therefore, make sure the way you use your energy today helps you move closer to your ideal future life. To do so, you need a clear vision and a sound strategy.

3. Allocate energy. You don't have enough energy to do everything at once. According to the 80/20 principle, twenty percent of your activities will generate eighty percent of your results. Using this principle, make sure you focus on the tasks that absolutely matter.

4. Invest energy. Your energy must be invested otherwise it will be lost. Once you've identified your key tasks, put all your energy into them while eliminating any distractions.

5. Refill energy. Take breaks regularly so as to maintain good energy levels.

6. Restart the cycle. You can then restart the cycle all over again the following day.

The point is, the more you can preserve energy and channel it toward the achievement of your most important goals, the more productive you'll become.

Now, let's go over the five levels of productivity to give you a better idea of how productivity works.

3. The five levels of productivity

Below is a quick overview of the five levels of productivity. Keep these levels in mind as you strive to make a better use of your time.

Level 1—destroying distractions and improving your focus

Level one is about eliminating distractions and putting your undivided attention into your major task.

Level 2—increasing your level of energy

Level two is about increasing your energy. To boost your productivity further, you must channel all your energy into the completion of your key task(s). This will enable you to inject more intensity into your time and to accomplish more as a result.

Level 3—clarifying your long-term vision

This level is about focusing on the correct things. You can complete as many tasks as you like, but if they don't move you closer to your goals, what's the point?

Level 4—planning your day effectively

This level is about optimizing your system and becoming a more effective planner. Through effective planning you can reduce distractions and increase the amount of focus you have available throughout the day.

Level 5—having an active social life and building meaningful relationships

The fifth level is about building meaningful relationships. How often and how well we interact with others has a big impact on our levels of productivity.

4. Productivity doesn't require complex systems

Write down what your current productivity system is (if you have one).

Is it working for you? If not, how can you make it simpler and more effective? Write down your answer below:

5. What is procrastination and how to overcome it

We usually procrastinate for the following reasons:

1. A lack of clarity
2. Insufficient awareness
3. Poor focus
4. Fear
5. Lack of urgency
6. Lack of effective routines
7. Unnecessary friction
8. Mental overload

Complete the exercise below to help you overcome procrastination"

1. Rate yourself on a scale from 1 to 10 (one being false, ten being true) for each statement below:

I lack clarity regarding what I need to do or how to do it.

0 _____ 10

I wait for motivation to arrive.

0 _____ 10

I'm distracted unable to complete hard tasks.

0 _____ 10

I'm afraid of not doing a good enough job.

0 _____ 10

I have no clear deadline or sense of urgency.

0 _____ 10

I have no daily routine to help me start work.

0 _____ 10

My environment encourages unproductive or toxic behaviors.

0 _____ 10

I have too many things to do, and I feel stuck.

0 _____ 10

2. Select one task you've been procrastinating on recently. Write it down below:

My task: _____

3. Write down the specific reason(s) you're procrastinating on this particular task (lack of clarity, insufficient awareness, poor focus, etc.).

4. Finally, write down one specific thing you could do to start that task.

PART II. UPDATE YOUR PERCEPTION OF TIME

1. Using past and future properly

A. Using your past effectively

Here are some ways you may misuse the past:

- You feel sorry about yourself for what happened in the past.
- You waste tons of energy trying to change things from the past.
- You feel ashamed or guilty for what you did in the past.
- You idealize your past.

Instead you can:

- Focus on all the things you did well.
- Remember times when you had courage.
- Give empowering meaning to negative events.
- Be self-compassionate.
- Practice letting go of difficult events.
- See your past as detached from your present.

Now, write down the specific ways you may be misusing your past.

Then, write down what you could focus on instead

B. Using your future effectively

Here are some ways you may misuse the future:

- worrying about a future event that hasn't happened yet
- focusing on all the things that could go wrong, and
- making future events into a much bigger deal than they really are.

Instead, you can

- Visualize your goals and get excited about them.
- Imagine future events going as you have already planned them. Think of all the ways things can go well in the future.
- Identify all the things that could go wrong.
- Avoid making future events a bigger deal than they probably are.

Write down below a few ways you're misusing your future.

Now, spend a few minutes visualizing yourself achieving your most exciting goals.

2. Using your present effectively

A. Be grateful for today

Start acknowledging your day using the provost below (or create your own):

- Thank you for this new day. I'll make the most of it.
- Today is a new opportunity to start afresh and let go of everything from the past.
- Today could very well be my last day. I'll act as if I hold my entire life in my hands.
- I'll make the most of today. By doing so, I know I'm building the best life possible.
- Today is always the most important day of my life, because it's the only day I have control over.

Write down one thing you could do every day to express your gratitude:

_____

Every day:

- Write down the date each morning and take a few seconds to acknowledge your day (using the prompts described earlier).
- Practice completing your key tasks through to the end.
- Try awareness, meditation and/or breathing exercises to calm your mind before working on your designated tasks (see below)

Awareness exercise

Below are some awareness exercises you can try:

- Isolate one sense and practice focusing on it for a moment (start with hearing for instance). Try to hear things you've never noticed before.
- Next, move your attention to another sense and do the same.

- Repeat this exercise for each sense (touch, sight, hearing, smell, and taste).
- Finally, try to be aware of all your senses at the same time.

Breathing exercises

Breath slowly, using the following frequency as mentioned by Gurucharan Singh Khalsa, Ph.D., and Yogi Bhajan, Ph.D. in their book, *Breathwalk*:

- Eight cycles per minute (offers relief from stress and increased mental awareness)
- Four cycles per minute (produces positive shifts in mental function, intense feelings of awareness, increased visual clarity, and heightened bodily sensitivity)

Meditating exercise.

Try this exercise as recommended by Brendon Burchard in *High Performance Habits*. A couple of minutes might be enough.

"Repeat the word 'release' in your mind over and over. As you do, command your body to release all the tension in your shoulders, in your neck in your face and jaw. Release the tension in your back and your legs. Release the tension in your mind and spirit. If this is hard, just focus on each part of your body, breathe deeply, and repeat the word 'release' in your mind."

2. Perceiving time as an investment

When you *invest* your time, you will utilize all your available energy and transform it into something valuable. For instance, you can transform your energy into:

- memories that will stay with you for the rest of your life
- skills that will serve you for years to come
- knowledge that will make you wiser and improve your life
- products or services that will allow you to express your creativity and serve others, and/or
- mental/physical well-being that enables you to maintain and increase your overall energy levels.

Review your typical week and complete the following exercises:

Write down one daily activity you would rate as being a poor use of your time (as opposed to being an investment).

Calculate the total number of hours you'll have spent on this activity over a lifetime (extrapolate assuming you'll live until 75). Write your answer below:

Write down the most exciting thing you could be doing instead. Don't limit yourself and write what you really, really want to do.

Then:

- Feel the pain and regret you'll experience from not having achieved this goal.
- Visualize yourself having achieved it. Get excited about it!
- Visualize how much progress you could make toward that exciting goal in the next year or the next decade if you free up the time by removing that single unproductive activity.

3. Understanding compound effect and long-term thinking

Complete the following exercises.

What is the one daily habit that would have the biggest impact on your productivity long-term if you were to implement it? Imagine what the impact would be if you stuck to it for the next five to ten years.

My one daily habit:

_____

Practice visualizing your long-term goals for a few minutes every day.

Develop the habit of acknowledging your small daily wins. Write down below what you could do to celebrate your wins.

To celebrate my win I will:

4. Creating urgency

Imagine you had only ninety days to achieve what you usually do in one full year. Feel the sense of urgency this creates and imagine how much more you'll achieve with such a mindset.

Now, choose one long-term goal and write it down below:

My one goal:

_____

Break it down into one ninety-day goal. Make sure it is a tangible goal you can picture. Make it a little challenging (to create urgency).

My ninety-day goal(s):

Then, add specific milestones by setting monthly and weekly goals.

My monthly goals:

My weekly goals:

Finally, write down what you need to do today to start making progress toward that goal.

Today's goal(s):

PART III. MAKING A MEANINGFUL USE OF YOUR TIME

1. The most dangerous five words you must stop using

Rate each statement below on a scale from 1 to 10 (one being false, ten being true):

I don't take full responsibility for my time.

0 _____ 10

I position myself as a victim, complaining I don't have time.

0 _____ 10

I fail to work on my goals because my reason isn't compelling enough.

0 _____ 10

I feel the need to look busy to fit in with others and avoid having to think more strategically.

0 _____ 10

Whenever you find yourself complaining you don't have time, do one of the following things:

- Say to yourself, "I choose not to make the time for this thing right now."
- Ask yourself, "How *can* I make the time for this thing?"

It will help you uncover your priorities.

2. Keeping a time log

Write down in detail all your daily activities for the next seven days. Make sure you include everything you do before, during, and after work.

Time Log
Day 1

Time	Activities

Day 2

Time	Activities

Day 3

Time	Activities

Day 4

Time	Activities

Day 5

Time	Activities

Day 6

Time	Activities

Day 7

Time	Activities

3. Being productive the right way

A. Fifteen key questions to help you gain clarity

a. Eliciting desire

1. What do I really, really want?

2. If I were to wake up tomorrow, completely alone without any family member, friend, or colleague to influence my decisions, what would I do differently?

3. If I were to be totally honest with myself, what would I start doing now? What would I stop doing?

4. If I was guaranteed to succeed in everything I do, where would I want to be in five years?

5. If I could spend my day exactly the way I wanted to, what would my ideal day consist of?

6. If I could focus only on doing one thing for the rest of my life, what would it be?

7. If I understood and truly believed I could achieve absolutely anything I wanted to, by sticking to it for long enough, what would I pursue in the next three to five years?

b. Finding your strengths and unique abilities

8. When am I the happiest at work and what am I doing?

9. What do I find so easy to do I genuinely wonder why others struggle to do the same thing?

10. What do people around me say I'm great at?

c. Uncovering your passion

11. What did I enjoy doing when I was a kid?

12. Who do I envy and why?

13. If I had all the time and money in the world, what would I do with it?

14. If I had complete confidence and were already my absolute best self, what would I be doing with my life?

15. How do I want to express myself to the world?

B. Characteristics of a good vision

Write down your vision while keeping in mind the point below (don't worry if it's still vague as you can refine it over time).

    a. It's exciting to you (obviously).
    b. It's crystal clear.

c. It is aligned with your values.

d. It allows you to feel alive and to express yourself the way you wish.

e. It pushes you to challenge yourself

My vision:

4. How to use your time well

When trying to assess how you use your time, keep in mind these 7 criteria:

1) Meaningful:

- Does the thing I work on have meaning to me? Does it align with my values, personality, or goals?
- Is the time I spend with this person or this group of people meaningful? Do I enjoy the conversation? Do I experience a sense of connection?
- Does what I do enable me to express my creativity? Does it nourish my soul? Does it make me come alive?

2) Enjoyable:

- Do I genuinely enjoy what I do?
- Is it fun? Does it make me smile or laugh?
- Does it help me relax?

3) Challenging:

- Is what I do challenging? Does it require me to move beyond my comfort zone and try things I've never tried before? Does it require me to stretch my current skills?
- Does it engage my creativity and my problem-solving skills?

4) Memorable:

- Does what I do create great memories I'll remember for years?
- Is it exciting or new?
- Is it playful or even somewhat silly?

5) Self-worth enhancing

- Does it enhance my self-worth?

- Does it build my character and improve me as a person?

6) Effective (For work/study)

- Is it the most effective way to approach my task or work on my goals, or could I do it more effectively?

7) Health enhancing

- Does it help me stay healthy or improve my health?

Look at all the activities you engage in during a typical day/week. (To help you, review the time log you created earlier.) Then, using the seven criteria described above, assess how much value you're actually gaining from each activity.

Finally, select one unproductive activity and replace it with a new more meaningful one. Write them down below:

Old activity:

New activity I'll replace it with:

PART IV. MAKING EFFECTIVE USE OF YOUR TIME

I. How to increase your time

A. Borrowing time

Make a list of ten friends, colleagues, or acquaintances you're the closest to.

Next to each name, write down what particular skills they possess.

Then, imagine that you could upload their brain directly into yours, and ask yourself what knowledge or skills would you like to receive from them?

Person	particular skills)

B. Thinking smartly

To think smartly:

- shorten your learning curve
- adopt a mastery mindset
- ask yourself empowering questions
- approach your tasks smartly, and
- Schedule thinking time.

Complete the exercises below:

Select one goal you'd most like to achieve.

My goal: _____

Shortening your learning curve

Now, write down what you could do to shorten the learning curve and reach it as quickly as possible.

Adopting a mastery mindset

Write down what you would do differently if you were to adopt a mastery mindset.

Asking yourself empowering questions

Come up with at least one question in each category and answer it ("What if", "How", and "Who").

Approach your task smartly

Choose one task and go through the seven-step process to approach it smartly (See "Approaching a task the correct way" at the end of this action guide)

Scheduling thinking time

Block thirty to sixty minutes this week to think.

2. Improving your skills

Write down the key skills you could learn or improve on in order to boost your productivity long term.

How could you use deliberate practice to improve your current skills or acquire new ones? Write your answers down below.

2. How to store time

A. Using money to store time

Write down below what you would do if you could store time (for example, retiring early, changing your career, dedicating more time to your hobbies, etc.):

What I would do If I could store time:

B. Becoming a smart consumer

Write down below a few things you'd like to buy

Then, calculate how many hours you must work to buy them

Finally, Write down alternative options below (Can you buy something less expensive while getting more or less the same benefits? Or should you merely give up on buying those things?)

3. Disconnecting time from money

A. Saving money vs. saving time

Write down all the ways you're giving more importance to money than to time. Then, write down what you would do differently if you perceived time as far scarcer than money.

I give more importance to money than time when:

If I perceived time as scarcer than money I would:

C. Leveraging your time

To master your time, you must learn to leverage it instead of selling it. Outlined below are the main things you can use to make more effective use of your time:

- Other people's time.
- Other people's money.
- Other people's knowledge.
- Other people's influence, or
- Technology.

Write down one important goal below. You can reuse the goal you wrote earlier.

My goal:

_____

Now, write down how your network could help you achieve this goal faster.

PART V. DEVELOPING EXTRAORDINARY FOCUS

1. The best productivity tool you'll ever have

The 80/20 Principle

Identify the twenty percent of your activities that bring eighty percent of your results. Then, write them down.

My 80/20 activities:

-

-

-

-

-

2. Developing focus

Create your daily routines following the step below:

1) Be at the same place, at the same time every day.

2) Have a trigger to kickstart your routine.

3) Decide the type of work you'll do.

4) Just start.

5) Commit.

My daily routine:

C. How to boost your ability to focus

Write down at least one specific thing you will do to sharpen your focus.

To sharpen my focus I will:

Additionally, to make it even easier to focus:

- Allow yourself to be bored to lower your stimulation level and tackle difficult and unappealing tasks more easily.
- Read more to develop your concentration.
- Batch minor tasks to free time to focus on your most important work.

- Take breaks frequently and deliberately to recharge your battery and increase your focus.
- Practice deep work whenever you have a few minutes during the day, and
- Never feel guilty but be self-compassionate instead.

3. Eliminating distractions

A. The distraction matrix and how to work distraction-free

During your day you can be distracted in mainly four different ways. That is, you can be:

1. Dragged,
2. Interrupted,
3. Seduced, and
4. Fooled.

Write down all the ways you're being dragged, interrupted, seduced, and fooled. Refer to the following grid.

B. Identify your biggest distraction

Make a list of the distractions you're a victim of for each type (dragged, interrupted, seduced, and fooled) using the table below

1. Dragged	2. Interrupted
Q: is this activity likely to derail me?	Q: is this hampering my activity to do focused work?
3. Seduced	**4. Fooled**
Q: Is this activity really what I should be doing now?	Q: Am I still looking for fancy productivity tools? Is my current system sustainable over the long term?

Now, underline the ones you tend to waste the most time on.

Identify the one activity with the biggest power to distract you and create a plan to eliminate it or reduce its impact.

Your biggest distraction:

How exactly you will eliminate it or reduce its impact:

C. CEO/COO/employee framework

Practice asking yourself the following questions at the start of each day:

CEO:

- Exactly what tasks do I need to complete today?

Employee:

- Do I know how to do the tasks?
- Do I have the skills/tools to complete them?
- Do I know why I need to do these tasks?
- Am I on board?
- Am I committed to doing them?
- If I feel inner resistance, what can I do to overcome it?

COO:

- What did I do well today?
- What could I have done better?
- What could be improved and exactly how?

Then, take a pen and piece of paper and write down the three main tasks you'd like to complete today and begin to work.

APPROACHING A TASK THE CORRECT WAY

Refer to this page before starting a new task. Alternatively, you can also print it out and put it on your desk.

Step 1. Prioritizing my task

- If I could do only one thing today, what task would have the most impact?
- Is this task moving me closer to my main goal?
- Do I really need to do it right now?

Step 2. Assessing the validity of my task

- Do I *really* need to do this task?
- Is right now the best timing?
- Do I work on it because I need to or because it makes me feel good?

Step 3. Clarifying what needs to be done

- What exactly do I need to do here?
- What does the finished product look like?

Step 4. Determining whether I should be the one doing it

- Is this task really worth my time?
- Is there anyone who could do it better than me? If so, can I ask for help?
- What would happen if I simply remove/postpone this task?
- Do I enjoy working on this task?

Step 5. Finding out the most effective way to tackle that task

- What tool(s) can I use, people can I ask or method can I rely on to complete that task as fast as possible?
- What skill could I learn or improve to complete this task faster in the future?

Step 6. Batching the task with other similar tasks

- Can I batch that task with other similar tasks?

Step 7. Automatizing/systematizing your task

- Can I create templates I can reuse every time I work on that task or similar ones?
- Can I create checklists?

THE 7 PILLARS OF THE MASTERY MINDSET

Pillar #1—Mastering repetition. To become truly adept at a skill, you must practice over and over until the skills become second nature. You must adopt the mindset that you will practice as many times as necessary until you achieve the results you want.

Pillar #2—Mastering the fundamentals. The most successful people on earth are obsessed with learning the fundamentals and there is a reason for this. Without strong fundamentals, your potential for growth is limited. Without the fundamentals, you can't become great, let alone world-class at whatever you do. Work on mastering the fundamentals.

Pillar #3—Having faith in the process. If you hire a coach, take a course or buy a book and believe it's *not* going to work, you've already lost half of the battle. You must have faith in the process and commit to doing whatever it takes to make it work for you.

. . .

Pillar #4—Being willing to learn. Your ability to humble yourself and to remain coachable is one of the keys to effective learning. The more personal responsibility you take for the results you achieve, the faster you will grow.

Pillar #5—Embracing long-term thinking. Masters always have a long-term plan. They know they cannot excel at anything without first spending years working on their craft. Make sure you think long term and make progress towards your goals each day.

Pillar #6—Being consistent. Consistency allows you to build momentum over time. It boosts your ability to focus, increases your self-esteem, and skyrockets your productivity. To become a master, simply start by doing something consistently every day, no matter how small the action may be.

Pillar #7—Focusing. When you fail to concentrate your attention on something that improves your life, you move away from the life you want to create. Eventually, what you focus on consistently day after day creates your life. So, make certain you get it right.

Printed in Great Britain
by Amazon

39010250R00136